Motivational Poems for Kids

MD Sharr

Published by pinky, 2024.

While every precaution has been taken in the preparation of this book, the publisher assumes no responsibility for errors or omissions, or for damages resulting from the use of the information contained herein.

MOTIVATIONAL POEMS FOR KIDS

First edition. July 23, 2024.

Copyright © 2024 MD Sharr.

ISBN: 979-8224223121

Written by MD Sharr.

Table of Contents

Preface 1
1. A Day in the Zoo 3
2. The Magic Treehouse 4
3. Space Adventure 5
4. The Brave Little Knight 7
5. Under the Sea 9
6. The Talking Toys 11
7. The Enchanted Garden 13
8. Dinosaur Friends 15
9. The Rainbow's End 17
10. A Day at the Circus 19
11. The Little Train That Could 21
12. A Picnic in the Park 23
13. The Lost Puppy 25
14. The Secret Library 27
15. The Friendly Ghost 29
16. The Time Machine 31
17. The Magic Paintbrush 33
18. The Giant's Garden 35
19. The Forest Fairies 37
20. The Friendly Giant's House 39
21. The Birthday Wish 41
22. The Pirate Treasure 43
23. The Friendly Dragon 45
24. The Musical Instruments 47
25. A Day on the Farm 49
26. The Magic Mirror 51
27. The Robot Friend 53
28. The Friendly Witch 55
29. The Jungle Safari 57
30. The Snow Day 59
31. The Magical School 61
32. The Balloon Ride 63

33. The Friendly Giant 65
34. The Butterfly Garden 67
35. The Mermaid's Tale 69
36. The Haunted House 71
37. The Magic Carpet 73
38. The Treasure Hunt 75
39. The Superhero Squad 77
40. The Secret Cave 79
41. The Friendly Alien 81
42. The Candy Factory 83
43. The Magic Shoes 85
44. The Flying Bicycle 87
45. The Princess and the Frog 89
46. The Secret Garden 91
47. The Animal Parade 93
48. The Pirate Ship 95
49. The Fairy Tale Land 97
50. The Knight's Quest 99
51. The Magic Spellbook 101
52. The Rainbow Unicorn 103
53. The Talking Cat 105
54. The Secret Island 107
55. The Friendly Ghosts 109
56. The Flying Castle 111
57. The Dragon's Egg 113
58. The Magic Cookbook 115
59. The Time Traveler 117
60. The Animal Rescue 119
61. The Fairy Godmother 121
62. The Wizard's Apprentice 123
63. The Mermaid Lagoon 125
64. The Treehouse Adventures 127
65. The Talking Books 129
66. The Secret Passage 131
67. The Magic Circus 133

68. The Friendly Monsters	135
69. The Little Mermaid	137
70. The Hidden Treasure	139
71. The Flying Bed	141
72. The Magic Wand	143
73. The Jungle Journey	145
74. The Snowy Adventure	147
75. The Moon Trip	149
76. The Robot Adventure	151
77. The Dragon's Tale	153
78. The Enchanted Castle	155
79. The Magic Forest	157
80. The Ghost's Secret	159
81. The Pirate's Map	161
82. The Starry Night	163
83. Memory updated	165
84. The Hidden Kingdom	167
85. The Magic Amulet	169
86. The Rainbow Bridge	171
87. The Animal School	173
88. The Secret Garden	175
89. The Dragon's Lair	177
90. The Magic Potion	179
91. The Enchanted Library	181
92. The Friendly Witch's House	183
93. The Pirate's Island	185
94. The Magic Seeds	187
95. The Talking Animals	189
96. The Hidden Treasure	191
97. The Magic Shoes	193
98. The Fairy Tale Castle	195
99. The Dragon's Friend	197
100. The Magic Paintings	199

Preface

Welcome to a world where imagination dances freely, where every page holds a new adventure, and where the power of words can light up the darkest corners of our hearts. This book, Motivational Poems for Kids, is crafted with love and a sprinkle of magic, dedicated to sparking joy, inspiration, and resilience in the young minds who hold it.

As we journey through childhood, we are constantly learning, growing, and discovering the world around us. Each day brings new challenges and triumphs, and through it all, the right words can make a difference. Poetry, with its rhythmic charm and expressive beauty, has a unique ability to capture our feelings, ignite our imaginations, and encourage us to strive for the stars.

In crafting these poems, my goal has been to create more than just verses. I aim to offer little windows into a world of wonder, where every poem serves as a guiding light, helping children navigate their dreams and daily experiences with confidence and joy. Whether it's finding courage in the face of a challenge, embracing creativity, or simply appreciating the magic of everyday moments, these poems are here to inspire and uplift.

Each poem is a reflection of the values and lessons that can shape a child's world. From the bravery of a friendly dragon to the enchantment of a magical forest, these poems are designed to resonate with the unique experiences and emotions of young readers. They celebrate the power of kindness, the thrill of adventure, and the beauty of learning and growing.

This collection is meant for every child who dreams big and every parent who wishes to nurture that dream. It's for teachers who seek to inspire their students, and for anyone who believes in the boundless potential of young hearts. Poetry has the power to reach across age and experience, to touch the soul, and to ignite a spark that can lead to incredible journeys.

As you read through these poems, I encourage you to take a moment to reflect on the messages and images they conjure. Let the words become a part of your daily life, infusing each day with a sense of wonder and possibility. Allow the verses to remind you that courage is not the absence of fear but the triumph over it, that creativity is a journey with endless paths, and that kindness is a gift we can all share.

In a world that often moves too quickly, where the noise of daily life can overshadow the quiet whispers of inspiration, this book is a small haven of peace and positivity. It is a reminder that within each of us lies a spark of magic, a wellspring of strength, and an unending potential to achieve great things.

The poems within these pages are crafted to be both entertaining and motivational, aiming to instill in young readers a sense of self-belief and a love for the beauty of words. They are designed to be read aloud, shared, and cherished, becoming a part of the cherished moments that families and friends share together.

So, dear reader, as you embark on this poetic journey, let the rhythm of these verses guide you. May they inspire you to dream big, to be brave, and to embrace every adventure with an open heart. Remember that the magic of poetry lies not just in the words themselves but in the feelings and dreams they inspire.

Thank you for joining me on this adventure. I hope that these poems bring as much joy and inspiration to your life as they have to mine in creating them. May they serve as a beacon of light and a source of motivation, reminding you always of the incredible power of imagination and the limitless potential that lies within.

With warmest wishes and endless dreams,

—**Author**

1. A Day in the Zoo

A Day in the Zoo, Oh what a view!
Monkeys swing high, under the sky,
Jumping from tree to tree, oh my!
With tails that twirl and faces so bright,
Their laughter fills the air with delight.
Next, we see lions, regal and strong,
With roars that echo all day long.
Golden manes that shimmer and shine,
In the warm sun, they look divine.
Graceful giraffes, so tall and grand,
With long necks that stretch across the land.
Nibbling leaves from the tallest trees,
They move with such calm and gentle ease.
Each animal with its special way,
Teaches us something new today.
From playful monkeys to lions brave,
To giraffes that in the treetops wave.
A day at the zoo, what fun we had,
Learning about creatures, makes us glad.
With every visit, there's more to see,
In this big, wonderful world of discovery.

Explanation:

This poem is about a child's day at the zoo, filled with excitement and wonder.
Monkeys: The child sees monkeys swinging from trees, their playful nature and cheerful faces make the child happy.
Lions: Next, the child observes the lions, admiring their strength and the beauty of their golden manes as they roar proudly.
Giraffes: The giraffes impress the child with their tall, elegant stature and how they eat leaves from high up in the trees.
The poem highlights the unique traits of each animal and shows how a visit to the zoo can be both fun and educational, sparking curiosity and joy in learning about the natural world.

2. The Magic Treehouse

In our backyard, a secret we found,
A magic treehouse that spins us around.
With a twist and a turn, and a flick of light,
It takes us to places of wonder and might.
First, we land on a pirate ship,
Where sails are high and swords are gripped.
Captain's hat on our heads, we shout,
"Ahoy, matey!" as we sail about.
Next, we're in an enchanted wood,
Where fairy tales come true, just like they should.
Unicorns prance and dragons fly,
Magic fills the air and the sky.
In each new land, a lesson we learn,
From courage to kindness at every turn.
Facing fears with hearts so bold,
Stories of wisdom, in our hearts, we hold.
With a twist and a turn, back home we go,
With tales of adventure that grow and grow.
The magic treehouse, our secret delight,
Brings us new dreams every night.

Explanation:

This poem tells the story of two friends who discover a magical treehouse in their backyard.
Pirate Ship: The treehouse first takes them to a pirate ship, where they experience the thrill of being pirates, shouting "Ahoy, matey!" and feeling brave.
Enchanted Wood: Next, they find themselves in an enchanted forest, filled with unicorns and dragons, where everything is magical and wondrous.
Through these adventures, the friends learn important lessons about courage, kindness, and facing their fears. The magic treehouse brings them back home, leaving them with exciting stories and dreams of future adventures. This poem shows that imagination and adventure can teach us valuable lessons and fill our lives with joy and wonder.

3. Space Adventure

In my rocket ship so fast,
Off to space, I zoom at last.
Through the sky, past the moon,
Stars above, a glowing tune.
Zero gravity, floating free,
I somersault so happily.
Twinkling lights in the night,
What a thrilling, wondrous sight!
Planets round, big and small,
I learn their names, I see them all.
Mercury, Venus, Earth so blue,
Mars, Jupiter, and Saturn too.
Uranus spins on its side,
Neptune's waves, a cosmic tide.
Pluto, tiny, far away,
All together, they dance and play.
Friendly aliens wave hello,
With smiles bright, their faces glow.
We share stories, we laugh and sing,
New friends made in a cosmic ring.
Back to Earth, my journey done,
A space adventure, oh what fun!
I learned so much among the stars,
In my rocket, I went so far.
Dreams of space in my heart stay,
A young astronaut, I'll find my way.
Exploring, learning, having fun,
My space adventure has just begun!

Explanation:
This poem tells the story of a young astronaut who embarks on an exciting journey through space.

Rocket Ship: The child takes off in a rocket ship, flying past the moon and marveling at the stars.

Zero Gravity: In space, they experience zero gravity, floating freely and enjoying the sensation.

Solar System: The astronaut visits all the planets, learning their names and unique characteristics.

Friendly Aliens: They meet friendly aliens who greet them warmly, share stories, and become new friends.

The journey ends with the young astronaut returning to Earth, filled with knowledge and joy from their space adventure. This poem encourages children to dream big, explore the universe, and embrace the wonders of learning.

4. The Brave Little Knight

In a kingdom far away,
Lived a knight, so small and brave each day.
With armor shiny, sword in hand,
He vowed to protect his homeland.
One day, a dragon fierce and grand,
Came to the kingdom, a threat at hand.
Breathing fire, it caused great fright,
But who would face this fearsome sight?
Up stepped the knight, so tiny and bold,
With a heart of courage, pure as gold.
"I may be small, but I'll stand tall,
To save my kingdom, I'll give my all!"
Through the forest, to the dragon's lair,
The little knight went, with utmost care.
He faced the beast with steady eyes,
Ready to conquer, no compromise.
"Great dragon, hear my plea,
Leave our kingdom, set us free."
The dragon roared, but saw the light,
In the brave heart of this little knight.
"You're braver than most, though you're so small,
Your courage and kindness, I see it all."
The dragon paused, then turned away,
And peace returned that very day.
The kingdom cheered, their hero hailed,
For even the smallest heart prevailed.
The brave little knight, forever known,
Proved that courage, in all sizes, is shown.

Explanation:
This poem is about a small knight who bravely faces a giant dragon to save his kingdom.

The Small Knight: The poem introduces a small but brave knight who is determined to protect his homeland.

The Dragon: A fierce dragon threatens the kingdom, causing fear among the people.

Facing the Dragon: Despite his small size, the knight courageously confronts the dragon, showing determination and bravery.

The Knight's Plea: The knight speaks to the dragon, asking it to leave the kingdom in peace.

The Dragon's Response: Impressed by the knight's courage and kindness, the dragon decides to leave, restoring peace to the kingdom.

The poem concludes with the kingdom celebrating their small knight's bravery, proving that true courage comes from within, regardless of size. This story encourages children to believe in themselves and understand that even the smallest acts of bravery can make a big difference.

5. Under the Sea

Under the sea, where wonders glow,
A child dives deep, with fins in tow.
In waters clear, so bright and blue,
A magical world comes into view.
Colorful fish swim all around,
In hues so bright, they do astound.
Striped and spotted, fast and slow,
A rainbow of fins puts on a show.
Playful dolphins leap with glee,
Their clicks and whistles calling me.
We dance and swirl in the ocean's play,
In the waves, we splash all day.
Wise old turtles, slow and grand,
Guide me gently with a flippered hand.
They tell tales of the ocean deep,
Of hidden caves where secrets sleep.
Coral reefs, so full of life,
With colors vibrant, sharp as a knife.
Anemones and sponges, bright and fair,
Tiny creatures everywhere.
Under the sea, there's so much to learn,
From every twist, and every turn.
Respect and wonder, these lessons grow,
In the depths where the currents flow.
With a heart full of joy, I swim back to shore,
Dreaming of oceans, and longing for more.
For under the sea, a world awaits,
Of beauty, friendship, and magical fates.

Explanation:
This poem tells the story of a child who dives underwater to explore the vibrant and magical world beneath the sea.

Diving Deep: The child starts their adventure by diving into the clear, blue ocean.

Colorful Fish: They encounter a variety of colorful fish, marveling at their bright patterns and movements.

Playful Dolphins: The child meets playful dolphins, who join them in a joyful dance in the waves.

Wise Old Turtles: They also meet wise old turtles, who guide them and share stories about the ocean's mysteries.

Coral Reefs: The child explores a vibrant coral reef, discovering the rich and diverse life it holds.

The poem emphasizes the beauty and wonder of the underwater world and teaches lessons of respect and curiosity for nature. It encourages children to explore, learn, and appreciate the magical environments around them.

6. The Talking Toys

In the playroom, quiet and still,
When no one's around, what a thrill!
The toys come to life, one by one,
Ready for adventures, full of fun.
Teddy Bear with his button nose,
Leads the way where magic flows.
Dolls and robots, cars and blocks,
Gather round in joyful flocks.
"Let's build a castle," says brave Knight,
"With Legos strong, it'll reach new height."
Princess Doll waves her wand so bright,
Adding sparkles to the night.
Race car zooms with a roaring sound,
Around the playroom, round and round.
"Watch out!" calls the robot tall,
"We need a bridge, so none will fall."
Stuffed giraffe with spots so neat,
Stretches high on his four feet.
"I'll help you reach those blocks up high,
Together we can touch the sky."
Puzzles come together with teamwork's might,
Pieces fitting left and right.
"We solve problems," shouts the toy crowd,
Working together makes us proud.
When morning comes, and day begins,
The toys go back with secret grins.
For in the night, they had their fun,
Adventures shared by everyone.
The talking toys, a playful crew,
Teach us lessons kind and true.
Friendship, teamwork, and joy so bright,
Come alive in the quiet night.

Explanation:

This poem is about toys in a playroom that come to life when no one is looking, embarking on adventures, and solving problems together.

Coming to Life: The toys come to life when the playroom is quiet and ready for fun and adventure.

Teddy Bear: The teddy bear leads the group, and all the toys gather around.

Building a Castle: The knight and princess doll, along with other toys, build a castle using Legos and add magical sparkles.

Race Car and Robot: The race car zooms around, and the robot helps solve the problem of needing a bridge.

Stuffed Giraffe: The giraffe helps by reaching high blocks, and demonstrating teamwork.

Puzzles and Teamwork: The toys work together to solve puzzles, showing the importance of teamwork.

When morning comes, the toys return to their places, having learned valuable lessons about friendship and teamwork. This poem encourages children to value cooperation and find joy in working together.

7. The Enchanted Garden

In a corner, behind the gate,
Lies a garden, truly great.
Hidden blooms and whispers bright,
Come alive in morning light.
A curious child, eyes open wide,
Steps into the magic inside.
Talking flowers, petals aglow,
Share their secrets, soft and slow.
"Welcome, friend," says Daisy tall,
"We're glad you've come to see us all."
"Look at me," says Rose so red,
"Feel my petals, soft as bed."
Butterflies flutter, colors bright,
In the enchanted garden's light.
Friendly insects, buzzing near,
Whispering secrets for the child to hear.
"I'm Bumblebee," with stripes of gold,
"I help flowers, strong and bold."
"And I'm Ladybug, spots so fine,
I keep the garden in a line."
Birds sing sweetly from the trees,
Dancing in the gentle breeze.
"This garden's magic," says the child,
Nature's wonders make me smile."
With every step, a new surprise,
A hidden world before their eyes.
Learning how the garden grows,
Nature's magic, the child now knows.
Back through the gate, the child does go,
With a heart that's learned to glow.
For in the garden, they did see,
The wonders of nature's harmony.

The enchanted garden, bright and true,
Teaches us what nature can do.
With talking flowers and insects kind,
A world of magic they did find.

Explanation:

This poem tells the story of a curious child who discovers an enchanted garden filled with talking flowers and friendly insects.

Entering the Garden: The child finds a hidden garden behind a gate and steps inside, discovering its magic.

Talking Flowers: The flowers in the garden, like Daisy and Rose, welcome the child and share their beauty.

Friendly Insects: Butterflies, bumblebees, and ladybugs introduce themselves and explain their roles in helping the garden thrive.

Birds and Magic: Birds sing from the trees, and the child feels the enchantment of the garden, appreciating the wonders of nature.

The poem highlights the beauty and magic of nature, teaching children to appreciate and learn from the natural world. It encourages curiosity and a sense of wonder, showing that there is much to discover and enjoy in nature.

8. Dinosaur Friends

In a time machine, zooming fast,
Back to the past, I've gone at last.
To a world of wonder, big and grand,
With dinosaurs in a prehistoric land.
First, I meet a Triceratops,
With three big horns and plant-filled chops.
"I eat greens," she says with pride,
"In the forests, I like to hide."
Next, a T-Rex with a mighty roar,
Stomping around, shaking the floor.
"I'm a hunter," he says with glee,
"Chasing prey is fun for me!"
Up in the sky, so high and free,
A Pterodactyl waves to me.
"With wings so wide, I soar above,
Flying is something that I love."
In the water, deep and cool,
A Plesiosaur swims like a jewel.
"I dive and glide, in lakes I stay,
Swimming through waters every day."
A Stegosaurus with plates so tall,
Shows me her back, sturdy and all.
"I use my tail for defense,
And live in herds, for common sense."
Through jungles thick and valleys wide,
I learn where these dinosaurs reside.
In different habitats, they thrive,
Each unique and so alive.
The sun sets down, it's time to go,
Back to my home, but now I know,
Dinosaurs, so grand and bright,
Fill my dreams with their might.

Dinosaur friends, I'll never forget,
The lessons learned, the fun we've met.
In their world, I've found the key,
To loving nature's history.

Explanation:

This poem is about a child who travels back in time to meet and learn about dinosaurs.

Time Machine: The child uses a time machine to travel to the prehistoric era.

Triceratops: The child meets a plant-eating Triceratops with three big horns.

T-Rex: Next, the child encounters a T-Rex, a powerful hunter with a mighty roar.

Pterodactyl: A Pterodactyl, a flying dinosaur, waves to the child from the sky.

Plesiosaur: The child sees a Plesiosaur swimming gracefully in the water.

Stegosaurus: Finally, the child meets a Stegosaurus with tall plates on its back, living in herds for protection.

The poem shows the child learning about different dinosaur species and their habitats. It ends with the child returning home, inspired by the dinosaurs and their unique characteristics. This poem encourages children to be curious about history and nature and to appreciate the diversity of life on Earth.

9. The Rainbow's End

One bright day after the rain,
A rainbow appeared, a colorful train.
Red, orange, yellow, and green,
A magical sight, so bright and serene.
I followed the rainbow, curious and bold,
To see where it led, and what I might hold.
Through meadows and forests, I made my way,
Chasing the colors, as they danced and played.
At the rainbow's end, oh what a sight,
A pot of gold, shimmering bright!
But who was there, with a twinkle in his eye,
A friendly leprechaun, small and spry.
"Welcome, young friend," he said with cheer,
"I guard this gold, but there's more here.
The real treasure," he grinned with pride,
"Is the happiness we find inside."
He shared with me his secrets so grand,
Of joy and laughter, a magical hand.
"Be kind and caring, spread joy around,
Happiness is where true gold is found."
"Help others and smile, each day anew,
With love in your heart, and dreams to pursue.
Gratitude and kindness, always hold dear,
These are the secrets, so crystal clear."
With a heart full of joy, I bid him goodbye,
The rainbow's end, a magical high.
The gold was lovely, but now I know,
True happiness comes from the love we show.
So, remember this tale, when you see a rainbow's gleam,
Happiness is more than a dream.
It's in the love we give and share,
That's where the true gold is found, everywhere.

Explanation:
This poem is about a child who follows a rainbow to its end and finds a pot of gold guarded by a leprechaun.

Following the Rainbow: After a rainy day, the child sees a rainbow and decides to follow it to see where it leads.

Pot of Gold: At the end of the rainbow, the child discovers a pot of gold.

Meeting the Leprechaun: A friendly leprechaun greets the child and shares the real secret of happiness.

Secrets of Happiness: The leprechaun explains that true happiness comes from kindness, love, and spreading joy.

Returning Home: The child leaves with a heart full of joy, understanding that the true treasure is the happiness found in giving and sharing love.

The poem teaches children that while material things are nice, the real value lies in kindness and the joy we bring to others. It encourages them to seek happiness in their actions and relationships.

10. A Day at the Circus

Under the big top, so high and wide,
The circus awaits with joy and pride.
A child walks in, eyes open wide,
To a world of wonder, where dreams reside.
Acrobats swing from the highest wire,
Twisting and turning, climbing higher.
With grace and skill, they soar through the air,
Performing magic, a sight so rare.
Clowns in bright colors, funny and loud,
Juggle and laugh, making the crowd proud.
Their big red noses and cheerful song,
Make everyone smile all day long.
Lions and tigers, so brave and grand,
Perform their tricks with a gentle hand.
Jumping through hoops and walking on cues,
They show their talents, and spread good news.
Elephants march in a grand parade,
With trumpeting sounds and a big parade.
Their majestic steps and swaying trunks,
Add to the fun and joyful plunks.
A cotton candy cloud, so sweet and pink,
A treat to enjoy, and just have a think.
Of all the wonders the circus can show,
A magical world where imagination grows.
As the sun sets and the lights go dim,
The circus ends with a joyful hymn.
With hearts full of wonder and eyes that gleam,
The child leaves with dreams and a magical dream.
For at the circus, all is bright,
Imagination takes flight.
With acrobats, clowns, and animals, too,
The magic of the circus comes alive for you.

Explanation:

This poem describes a day at the circus, showcasing the excitement and wonder experienced by a child.

Entering the Circus: The child arrives at the circus, amazed by the grand, colorful spectacle.

Acrobats: The acrobats perform incredible aerial feats, soaring through the air with skill.

Clowns: The clowns entertain with their funny antics, making everyone laugh and smile.

Trained Animals: Lions, tigers, and elephants perform tricks, showing their talents with the help of their trainers.

Cotton Candy: The child enjoys sweet cotton candy, adding to the fun of the day.

Leaving the Circus: As the day ends, the child leaves with a heart full of joy and imagination, inspired by the magic of the circus.

The poem highlights the joy and inspiration found at the circus, encouraging children to use their imagination and appreciate the wonders of creativity and performance.

11. The Little Train That Could

In a valley, green and wide,
A little train sat by the side.
With a whistle and a chug, so small and bright,
It dreamed of reaching a towering height.
A steep hill rose, so tall and grand,
The little train could hardly stand.
"Can I make it up?" it asked with hope,
"Or will I find it hard to cope?"
"I think I can," it said with cheer,
"I'll give it my best, and never fear."
With wheels a-turning and engine loud,
The little train chugged, feeling proud.
Up the hill, with grit and might,
The little train climbed, day and night.
Its puffing steam and steady pace,
Brought a smile to its little face.
Other trains, so big and strong,
Watched and cheered along the throng.
"Keep going, little train, don't stop now,
With every chug, you'll make it somehow!"
Higher and higher, it reached the crest,
With a burst of joy, it took a rest.
"I knew I could," it said with pride,
"Believing in myself was the ride."
Down the hill, it rolled with glee,
Happy and free, as proud as can be.
The little train showed, in every way,
That with perseverance, you can sway.
So when you face a hill so steep,
Remember the little train's leap.
Believe in yourself, keep chugging through,
And you'll find success waiting for you.

Explanation:

This poem is about a small train that faces the challenge of climbing a steep hill and learns the value of perseverance and self-belief.

Starting Point: The little train is small but dreams of climbing a tall hill.

Determination: Despite doubts, the train decides to try its best and stay positive.

Climbing the Hill: The train works hard, moving slowly but steadily up the hill with encouragement from others.

Reaching the Top: The train successfully reaches the top, feeling proud of its accomplishment.

Rolling Down: The train enjoys the ride down, knowing that believing in itself made the journey possible.

The poem teaches children that persistence and self-belief can help overcome challenges. It encourages them to keep trying, no matter how difficult a task may seem.

12. A Picnic in the Park

On a sunny day, so warm and bright,
Friends gather for a picnic, what a delight!
With a blanket spread on the soft green grass,
They laugh and play as the hours pass.
Kites soar high, up in the sky,
As children run and cheer with a joyful cry.
Games of tag and hide-and-seek,
Bring out smiles on every cheek.
A basket filled with treats so sweet,
Sandwiches, cookies, and fruit to eat.
Juice and lemonade, chilled and nice,
Refreshing sips and a tasty slice.
They sit and chat, sharing stories old,
In the park where the sun is bold.
Birds sing songs, and flowers sway,
Making the park a magical place to play.
A gentle breeze whispers through the trees,
As friends enjoy their day with ease.
The joy of nature, simple and true,
Makes their hearts feel fresh and new.
As the sun begins to set, so low,
They pack up their things, and slowly go.
With memories made of laughter and cheer,
They leave the park, happy and near.
For in the park, with friends so dear,
They learned that simple joys bring cheer.
A day with nature, games, and fun,
Is a day to cherish, when all is said and done.

Explanation:
This poem describes a delightful picnic in the park with friends, showcasing the simple joys of spending time outdoors.

Picnic Setup: Friends come together for a picnic on a sunny day, spreading a blanket on the grass.

Games and Fun: They play games like kite flying, tag, and hide-and-seek, enjoying each other's company.

Delicious Treats: They eat from a basket filled with tasty treats such as sandwiches, cookies, and lemonade.

Nature's Beauty: They appreciate the park's beauty, including the birds, flowers, and gentle breeze.

Ending the Day: As the day ends, they pack up and leave, cherishing the memories of a joyful day spent in nature.

The poem highlights the fun and happiness found in simple activities and spending time with friends, encouraging children to enjoy and appreciate the little moments in life.

13. The Lost Puppy

On a bright and sunny day so fine,
A child found a puppy, lost and in a bind.
With big brown eyes and a tiny tail,
The puppy looked worried, sad, and frail.
"Don't worry, little friend," the child said with a grin,
"We'll find your home, let the journey begin."
They walked through the park and down the lane,
Calling the puppy's name in the sunshine and rain.
"Is this your house?" asked the child with care,
But the puppy just looked and shook its hair.
"Let's try another," the child said with hope,
They continued their search, learning how to cope.
They asked their neighbors, "Have you seen this pup?"
With kind hearts and smiles, they never gave up.
Finally, a kind woman came with delight,
"I've been looking for my puppy all night!"
The puppy's tail wagged, it jumped with cheer,
The child smiled wide, happy to hear.
The puppy was home, safe and sound,
Thanks to the kindness that was found.
The child learned a lesson, oh so true,
That helping others is what we should do.
Kindness and care, a little responsibility,
Can make a big difference, that's the key.
So, remember this tale when you see someone lost,
A little help and kindness is worth any cost.
With a heart full of love and a helping hand,
You can make the world a better land.

Explanation:
This poem tells the story of a child who finds a lost puppy and helps it find its way home, learning about kindness and responsibility.
Finding the Puppy: The child finds a lost puppy looking sad and scared.

Helping the Puppy: The child decides to help the puppy find its home, searching through the park and asking neighbors.

Finding the Owner: A kind woman recognizes the puppy and happily reunites with it.

Lesson Learned: The child learns that helping others and showing kindness are important and valuable.

The poem teaches children that being kind and responsible can make a big difference in someone's life. It encourages them to help others and shows that small acts of kindness are very meaningful.

14. The Secret Library

In a quiet corner, hidden and deep,
A secret library begins to sleep.
Behind a door with a golden key,
Books wait quietly for you and me.
A child finds the key and turns it with care,
Unlocking a world of wonders rare.
With a creak, the door opens wide,
And adventures within come alive and glide.
The first book whispers, "Come take a ride,"
And the child steps in with eyes open wide.
They sail on a ship through an ocean of blue,
With pirates and treasure, a magical view.
Another book calls, "Let's fly to the sky!"
And the child soars high, up in the clouds so high.
Meeting dragons and stars, and a moonlit race,
Every page turns into a new, thrilling place.
A third book reveals a land so grand,
Where talking animals play in the sand.
The child joins in, with laughter and cheer,
Making friends with creatures, far and near.
With each new story, the child learns and grows,
In a world where imagination flows.
The library's magic, both fun and wise,
Shows how adventures can open your eyes.
When the child leaves and locks the door tight,
They carry the magic, warm and bright.
For in the secret library, dreams take flight,
And every book is a new, dazzling light.
So find your own key, explore far and wide,
Let your imagination be your guide.
In every story, new worlds you'll find,
With magic and adventure, expanding your mind.

Explanation:

This poem is about a hidden library where books come to life, taking a child on exciting adventures.

Discovering the Library: A child finds a hidden library and unlocks it with a special key.

Adventures Begin: The books in the library come to life, leading the child on various adventures such as sailing with pirates, flying with dragons, and playing with talking animals.

Learning and Growing: Each adventure helps the child learn and grow, showing how imagination can open new worlds.

Leaving the Library: As the child leaves, they take the magic and excitement of the library with them.

The poem encourages children to explore their imagination and see the magic in books and stories. It highlights how reading can lead to amazing adventures and personal growth.

15. The Friendly Ghost

In a house that's old and creaky,
With walls that whisper and floors that squeaky,
Lived a ghost with a gentle smile,
Who greeted each visitor with a friendly style.
Though the house was known to be quite spooky,
The ghost inside was anything but kooky.
With a soft, glowing light and a friendly wave,
He showed no fear, was kind and brave.
One night, some children dared to explore,
The old house's mystery, legends, and lore.
With flashlights in hand and hearts that beat fast,
They entered the house, hoping the fright would not last.
But instead of a scare, they saw a warm glow,
The friendly ghost greeted them with a bow.
"Welcome, dear friends, to my humble abode,
There's no need to fear, this is a friendly mode!"
He showed them around with a twinkle in his eye,
His laughter like music, making the night fly.
The children learned as they walked through the halls,
That not everything spooky is scary at all.
The ghost played games and shared some sweet treats,
He told them fun stories and showed them the sweets.
By the end of the night, they were happy and wise,
Understanding the ghost was a kind, pleasant surprise.
As they left, they waved and said goodbye,
Grateful for the friend who made them feel high.
They learned not to fear what's unknown or strange,
For kindness can come in the most unexpected range.
So if you encounter something that seems quite unclear,
Remember the ghost and don't give in to fear.
Sometimes what's scary is just misunderstood,
And a friendly face can turn fright into good.

Explanation:
This poem tells the story of a friendly ghost living in a spooky house who teaches children not to fear the unknown.

The Friendly Ghost: The ghost in the old house is kind and welcoming, not scary.

Children Explore: Brave children enter the spooky house, expecting to be frightened.

Meeting the Ghost: Instead of a scare, they find the ghost friendly, who shows them around and shares treats.

Learning and Farewell: The children learn that not everything spooky is to be feared and that kindness can be found in unexpected places.

The poem encourages children to face their fears with an open mind and to understand that things that seem frightening may turn out to be friendly and kind. It highlights the importance of not letting fear prevent them from discovering new and positive experiences.

16. The Time Machine

In a cozy room with a gentle light,
A child finds a time machine one night.
With a twist of the dial and a whoosh so grand,
They're whisked away to a magical land.
First, they land in days of old,
Where knights and castles are stories told.
A brave knight smiles and says, "Hello,"
Teaching courage and honor, so the child would know.
Next, they visit a world of art and fame,
Where a painter named Picasso made a name.
"Creativity is key," he said with a grin,
"Let your imagination be where you begin."
The machine whirls on with a shimmering hue,
To a land of pyramids and skies so blue.
A wise old Pharaoh shares his ancient view,
"Respect and knowledge are treasures too."
Onward to a bustling, modern town,
Where a scientist in a lab wears a frown.
"Never give up," says the scientist with cheer,
"Failures are just steps to success, my dear."
Back to the machine, with hearts so full,
The child returns, feeling quite cool.
They've learned from the past and seen the old,
That lessons from history are worth more than gold.
So remember this tale when you dream and play,
History's lessons can light up your way.
Courage, creativity, respect, and trying your best,
Are secrets from the past that will help you in your quest.
With the time machine's magic, you've seen it's true,
That learning from the past helps you start anew.
Explanation:

This poem is about a child who travels through time in a magical time machine, meeting famous historical figures and learning valuable lessons.

Discovering the Time Machine: The child finds a time machine and travels through different historical periods.

Meeting Historical Figures: The child meets a knight who teaches about courage, an artist who values creativity, a Pharaoh who values respect and knowledge, and a scientist who encourages perseverance.

Returning Home: The child returns home with important lessons learned from the past, feeling inspired.

The poem encourages children to learn from history and see the value in lessons from the past. It teaches that qualities like courage, creativity, respect, and perseverance are timeless and can guide them in their own lives.

17. The Magic Paintbrush

In a room full of colors and brushes so bright,
A child found a brush that sparkled with light.
With a swish and a stroke, and a magical flair,
The brush made the child's dreams float in the air.
First, they painted a sun with a big, wide grin,
And out it popped, shining bright from within.
It danced in the sky and warmed up the day,
Spreading sunshine in every way.
Next came a cat with fur of rainbow hues,
It purred and played, making friends with the shoes.
The child laughed as the cat did a twirl,
Making everyone smile, every boy and girl.
A house was painted with colors so bold,
And out came a giant, made of gingerbread and gold.
It winked and it waved, and said with delight,
"Come in for a party, we'll have fun all night!"
A dragon was painted with scales so bright,
It soared through the air with a mighty flight.
But when it landed, it hiccupped with grace,
Blowing out bubbles all over the place.
The child had so much fun, painting each scene,
From a dancing elephant to a jellybean queen.
Each stroke of the brush brought laughter and cheer,
Creating a world where joy was near.
As the day ended, the brush sparkled and sighed,
The magic would rest, but the fun never died.
For in the child's heart, the adventures stayed,
In a world full of colors, where dreams were displayed.
So remember this tale of the magical brush,
Imagination can make your world sparkle and rush.
With a touch of creativity and a dash of delight,
You can bring your dreams to life, shining so bright.

Explanation:

This poem is about a child who discovers a magical paintbrush that brings whatever they paint to life, creating fun and imaginative situations.

Finding the Magic Brush: The child finds a special brush that makes their paintings come alive.

Magical Paintings: The child paints a smiling sun, a rainbow-colored cat, a gingerbread house, and a friendly dragon, each creating joyful and humorous scenes.

Joy and Imagination: The magical brush brings happiness and laughter, making the child's world full of wonder.

Ending and Lesson: As the day ends, the magic of the brush rests, but the fun and creativity remain in the child's heart.

The poem encourages children to use their imagination and creativity, showing that with a bit of fantasy, they can create a world full of joy and wonder.

18. The Giant's Garden

In a land where the tall grass grows,
And a giant's old garden no longer glows,
The flowers were wilting, the trees were bare,
The garden looked tired, but children did care.
One sunny day, the children arrived,
With buckets and spades, they were eager and alive.
They saw the giant, who was feeling quite sad,
His garden was dusty and looking so bad.
"Let's make it bloom!" the children declared,
With smiles and excitement, they all gladly shared.
They watered the flowers, pulled weeds with delight,
And soon the garden started looking so bright.
They planted new seeds in neat little rows,
And gave every tree a gentle, warm dose.
The giant watched with a tear in his eye,
As his garden awoke beneath the blue sky.
The flowers stretched out, the trees began to sway,
The garden transformed in a magical way.
With colors and scents, and butterflies too,
It became a paradise, all shiny and new.
The giant was thrilled, his heart full of cheer,
He thanked the children with a great big, loud cheer.
The garden was saved, and so was the day,
All thanks to teamwork, and the children's way.
So remember this story, let it show you how,
Teamwork can turn things around, starting now.
With friends by your side and a heart full of care,
You can make magic happen anywhere.

Explanation:
This poem tells the story of a neglected garden owned by a giant, which is transformed into a beautiful paradise by a group of children working together.
Neglected Garden: The giant's garden is in poor condition, making him sad.

Children's Help: Children arrive and decide to help by cleaning, planting, and nurturing the garden.

Garden's Transformation: With their hard work and teamwork, the garden blooms into a vibrant and beautiful place.

Giant's Gratitude: The giant is very grateful, and the children's teamwork has made a big difference.

The poem teaches the value of teamwork and shows that working together with kindness and care can achieve wonderful results. It encourages children to collaborate and support each other to bring about positive changes.

19. The Forest Fairies

In a forest deep, where the tall trees sway,
A child found fairies, dancing at play.
With wings that sparkled in the dappled light,
They twirled and sang from morning till night.
"Welcome!" they cheered, with a gentle breeze,
"Come learn from us and explore with ease."
The fairies showed the child flowers so rare,
And the magic of nature they learned to share.
"See the tall trees and the soft green moss,
Each little leaf is a treasure, not lost.
The river's song and the bird's sweet cheer,
Are gifts from nature that we hold dear."
The child watched in awe as the fairies flew,
Through a forest where the air felt fresh and new.
They pointed to stars twinkling in the sky,
And the moon's gentle light as it sailed by.
"We must protect this land, so beautiful and grand,
Keep it clean and safe, it's our gift to the land.
For nature is precious, a treasure so fine,
And caring for it is truly divine."
The child nodded with a heart full of grace,
Understanding the beauty of this special place.
They promised to help and keep the forest bright,
To honor the fairies and their world of light.
So remember this tale, let it guide your way,
Protect nature's wonders each and every day.
With love and respect for the world all around,
You'll find magic and joy that's truly profound.

Explanation:
This poem is about a child who meets fairies in a forest and learns about the beauty of nature and the importance of protecting the environment.

Meeting the Fairies: The child encounters fairies in the forest who are dancing and playing.

Learning About Nature: The fairies teach the child about the wonders of nature, including trees, flowers, rivers, and the sky.

Importance of Protection: The fairies emphasize the need to take care of the environment and keep it clean and safe.

Commitment to Help: The child promises to protect the forest and honor the fairies' teachings.

The poem encourages children to appreciate and care for nature, showing that by protecting the environment, they can preserve the beauty and magic of the world around them.

20. The Friendly Giant's House

In a land where hills were big and tall,
Stood a giant's house, big enough for all.
With windows round and a door so wide,
It looked so cozy from the outside.
One sunny day, with hearts so bright,
A group of kids came into sight.
They saw the giant's house with awe,
And wondered what adventures it saw.
The door creaked open with a friendly sound,
And out stepped the giant, so gentle and round.
"Hello, small friends!" he said with cheer,
"Come inside and see what's here!"
The giant's house was a sight to see,
With furniture made just for him and me.
A chair as big as a mountain top,
And a table where giant flowers pop.
In the kitchen, pots and pans were huge,
But the giant cooked with love and a gentle mood.
He made pancakes that were fluffy and sweet,
And shared them with the children for a special treat.
The giant had a garden, oh so grand,
With flowers and veggies that seemed to expand.
He showed the kids how to plant and grow,
And how kindness in every seed will show.
They played with toys that were big and bright,
And danced with shadows in the soft moonlight.
The giant told stories of lands afar,
And of friends who shone like every star.
When the day ended, and the sun grew low,
The children felt a warm, happy glow.
For the giant's house had shown them the way,
That kindness and wonder brighten every day.

So when you meet someone big or small,
Remember that kindness can be a gift to all.
In every smile and every kind deed,
You'll find the beauty that we all need.

Explanation:

The poem "The Friendly Giant's House" describes a magical visit to a giant's house, which teaches valuable lessons about kindness and wonder:

Approaching the House: A group of children arrives at the giant's house, amazed by its size.

Meeting the Giant: The giant greets them warmly and invites them inside.

Exploring the House: The house is full of giant furniture and lovely surprises.

Sharing a Meal: The giant cooks and shares delicious pancakes with the children.

Gardening Together: The giant shows the children how to garden, teaching them about growth and kindness.

Playing and Stories: They play with giant toys and listen to wonderful stories.

Lessons Learned: The children learn that kindness and a sense of wonder make every day brighter.

The poem encourages children to appreciate the kindness of others and to find beauty and joy in unexpected places.

21. The Birthday Wish

On a special day, with cake and cheer,
A child made a wish as their birthday drew near.
They closed their eyes and whispered so low,
"I wish for a journey where magic will show."
In a flash of sparkles and twinkling light,
The child found themselves in a land so bright.
The sky was a canvas of rainbow hues,
With clouds that danced and soft, gentle tunes.
A friendly dragon with wings so grand,
Invited the child to explore the land.
They soared through the air and touched the stars,
Chasing moonbeams and Jupiter's scars.
They landed on islands made of candy and cream,
Where fairies and unicorns danced in a dream.
The child joined the fun with a joyful heart,
Feeling like they were a magical part.
They sailed on a ship with sails of gold,
Through oceans of dreams where stories unfold.
They met wise wizards and playful sprites,
And learned that dreams can reach new heights.
As the journey ended, the child made a vow,
To always believe in the magic somehow.
For each birthday wish, big or small,
Can take you on adventures, one and all.
So remember this tale when your day comes near,
Make a wish with a heart full of cheer.
For magic and wonder are always in sight,
Waiting to dance in the birthday light.

Explanation:

This poem is about a child who makes a birthday wish that takes them on a magical journey.
Making the Wish: On their birthday, the child wishes for a magical adventure.

Magical Journey: The child finds themselves in a colorful, magical land where they meet a friendly dragon and explore wonderful places.

Fantastic Experiences: They enjoy various fantastical experiences, like flying through the stars, dancing with fairies, and sailing on a golden ship.

Believing in Magic: The child learns that believing in magic and making wishes can lead to amazing adventures.

The poem inspires children to dream big and believe in the magic of their wishes, showing that even on ordinary days, special adventures can happen if you just believe.

22. The Pirate Treasure

In a dusty old chest, a map was found,
With clues to a treasure buried underground.
Three friends with a gleam in their eyes so bright,
Set sail on an adventure, from morning till night.
With a compass in hand and a sail full of wind,
They followed the map where the X marks the end.
Through stormy seas and over waves that roar,
Their ship cut through waters as they explored.
They climbed up tall mountains and trekked through the sand,
They solved tricky riddles with a steady hand.
With every step closer, their hearts beat fast,
They wondered what treasure they'd find at last.
At the end of their journey, the X was revealed,
A hidden chest, shiny and sealed.
They opened it wide, their eyes full of glee,
And found not gold, but a note that said, "See?"
"The greatest treasure you've found along the way,
Is the friendship you've built and the fun of the day.
For sharing adventures, and laughter so grand,
Is the real treasure, more precious than gold in the sand."
So remember this tale, when you're seeking a prize,
It's the friends you make and the joy in your eyes.
For the true treasure in life is always clear,
It's the friendships you cherish, year after year.

Explanation:
This poem tells the story of three friends who embark on a pirate adventure to find treasure, only to discover that their true treasure is the friendship they share.
Finding the Map: The friends find a treasure map and set out on an adventurous journey.
Adventure and Challenges: They face various challenges, such as storms, riddles, and rough terrains.

Discovering the Treasure: At the end of their journey, they find a chest with a note inside instead of gold.

Value of Friendship: The note reveals that the real treasure is the friendship and fun they had during the adventure.

The poem teaches that the true value in life is the relationships and shared experiences we have with others, rather than material possessions.

23. The Friendly Dragon

In a quiet village, not far from here,
Lived a dragon so gentle, with eyes full of cheer.
But his scales were green and his roar was loud,
So the villagers hid, they were scared of the sound.
"He's just a big monster!" the townsfolk would say,
"We must keep our distance, and stay far away."
But the dragon was kind and never meant harm,
He just wanted to help with his magical charm.
One day a storm came with thunder and rain,
And the village was worried, feeling the strain.
The dragon saw their trouble, their homes in dismay,
And decided to help in his own special way.
With a mighty flap of his big, friendly wings,
He flew to the village and did wonderful things.
He carried the children from rooftops so high,
And warmed up their homes with a fire that's dry.
The villagers watched in amazement and awe,
As the dragon worked hard without a single flaw.
They saw his big heart and the love that he gave,
And realized their fear had been terribly grave.
"He's not just a dragon," they joyfully cried,
"He's a hero who's caring and never would hide.
Let's welcome him warmly, and give him a cheer,
For true friendship is what we hold dear."
Now the village is happy, with the dragon in tow,
They learned that acceptance can help friendships grow.
So remember this tale of the dragon so kind,
And look past appearances to what's truly behind.

Explanation:
This poem is about a dragon who is misunderstood by a village due to his appearance but later becomes their hero, teaching them about acceptance and looking beyond outward appearances.

Misunderstood Dragon: The dragon is initially feared because of his roar and green scales.

Helping in a Storm: When a storm hits, the dragon helps the villagers by rescuing children and keeping their homes warm.

Villagers' Realization: The villagers see the dragon's kindness and realize their fear is unfounded.

Acceptance: They welcome the dragon as a hero and learn that true friendship comes from understanding and accepting others.

The poem encourages children to look beyond appearances and understand that kindness and heroism come in many forms, teaching the value of acceptance and the importance of seeing the true heart of others.

24. The Musical Instruments

In a grand concert hall, where music plays loud,
Instruments rested, as quiet as a cloud.
But when the moonlight touched every shiny key,
The instruments woke up, excited and free!
The trumpet, so bright, with its golden gleam,
Hopped up and said, "Let's start the dream!"
The strings picked up their bows with flair,
And the drums gave a beat with rhythm to share.
The violin danced with its soft, graceful song,
While the piano's keys played a tune so strong.
The flute flitted like a butterfly in flight,
And the tuba rumbled deep, with all its might.
They played a symphony that sparkled like stars,
Each note like a rainbow, from Venus to Mars.
The music swirled like a magical breeze,
Lifting the hearts of those who'd listen with ease.
The instruments knew their tunes were a treasure,
Each one with a part that brought joy and pleasure.
Together they showed how their melodies blend,
Creating a magic that never would end.
So remember this tale when you hear a new sound,
Each note and each rhythm has magic profound.
With harmony and friendship, together we shine,
And create music that's wonderfully divine.

Explanation:

This poem tells the story of musical instruments in an orchestra coming to life and making beautiful music together.

Instruments Wake Up: At night when the moonlight touches them, the instruments come alive and get excited.

Playing Together: Each instrument, from the trumpet to the violin, starts playing its part, creating a joyful and magical symphony.

Magical Music: The music they make is described as sparkling and magical, showing how each instrument contributes to a beautiful harmony.

Lesson in Harmony: The poem teaches that music is a wonderful combination of different sounds, and working together can create something magical and special.

The poem encourages children to appreciate the unique contributions of each person or thing, showing how working together and combining talents can create something extraordinary and magical.

25. A Day on the Farm

Wake up to sunshine and a rooster's crow,
It's time for a farm visit, so let's go!
With boots on our feet and a smile so wide,
We'll explore the farm and enjoy the ride.
First, we see the cows with their big, brown eyes,
Munching on grass under wide-open skies.
They give us fresh milk, so creamy and sweet,
A tasty treat we're lucky to eat.
Next, we visit the hens and their cozy coop,
With eggs for breakfast, ready to scoop.
The chickens are clucking and flapping around,
In their happy home, where they've safely found.
The pigs are rolling in mud with glee,
Splashing and playing so happily.
They love their cool puddles and their squishy fun,
In their muddy playground under the sun.
We help with the crops, planting seeds in a row,
Watering and watching as the plants start to grow.
The farm is a place where the green things bloom,
And we learn how they thrive with room to zoom.
At the end of the day, as the sun starts to fade,
We say goodbye to the farm we've enjoyed and played.
With memories of animals and farm life so grand,
We leave with a smile and a wave of the hand.
So remember this day and the fun that we had,
The farm teaches us things that make us feel glad.
From cows to chickens and pigs that play,
It's a beautiful place where we learn and stay.

Explanation:
This poem describes a fun and educational visit to a farm, showcasing various farm activities and animals.

Starting the Visit: The day begins with excitement and the anticipation of exploring the farm.

Meeting the Animals: The children encounter different animals like cows, chickens, and pigs, each with their unique characteristics and contributions.

Farm Activities: They engage in farm activities like collecting eggs, playing with pigs, and planting seeds.

Enjoying the Experience: As the day ends, they reflect on the enjoyable experience and the beauty of farm life.

The poem highlights the simple joys of rural life and teaches children about farm animals and activities, emphasizing the value of hands-on learning and appreciating the natural world.

26. The Magic Mirror

In a cozy old room with a mirror so bright,
A child found a secret one magical night.
When they looked in the glass, they saw something new,
A world full of wonders and adventures to pursue.
The mirror shimmered and swirled with a gleam,
Showing magical lands like a wondrous dream.
First, they stepped into a forest of gold,
Where animals talked and stories were told.
The wise old owl perched high in the tree,
Said, "Kindness and courage are the keys, you see."
The child learned to help and to always be brave,
In every adventure, kindness they gave.
Next, they flew to a castle up high,
With a dragon who danced and soared through the sky.
The dragon roared with a joyful cheer,
Teaching the child not to give in to fear.
Then, a trip to the sea with a ship made of shells,
Led to a treasure of stories and magical spells.
The child learned that the best treasure of all,
Is the joy and the fun in the adventures we call.
As the mirror's magic began to fade,
The child saw their room and felt unafraid.
They knew that the lessons were real and so true,
That bravery and kindness would always see them through.
So remember this tale when you face something new,
With courage and kindness, there's nothing you can't do.
For the magic you seek is not far away,
It's in your own heart, guiding your way.

Explanation:
This poem tells the story of a child who discovers a magic mirror that reveals different magical worlds and adventures, each teaching valuable life lessons.

Discovering the Magic Mirror: The child finds a mirror that shows magical worlds when they look into it.

Adventures and Lessons: The child visits various magical lands, where they learn important lessons from wise characters, such as kindness, courage, and the true value of joy and fun.

Returning Home: As the magic fades, the child returns to their room, feeling empowered by the lessons learned.

Life Lessons: The poem emphasizes that the real magic is found in one's own heart and the values of bravery and kindness.

The poem encourages children to embrace new experiences with a positive attitude and to recognize that the lessons they learn can help them navigate their own lives with confidence and compassion.

27. The Robot Friend

In a garage so tidy and full of delight,
A child found a robot one magical night.
With shiny, sleek metal and eyes that would glow,
The robot blinked twice and said, "Hello!"
"I'm Robo," it buzzed with a cheerful beep,
"Let's explore and discover, no time for sleep!"
Together they ventured to places so grand,
In a world full of tech, full of wonders so grand.
They built flying drones that zoomed through the air,
And created cool gadgets beyond all compare.
Robo showed how circuits and gears make things move,
With lights and with sounds that sparkle and groove.
They painted with lasers, and danced with a bot,
Made robots that played games and told jokes on the spot.
Every day was an adventure with new things to try,
Their imaginations soared, reaching the sky.
The child learned that creativity has no bounds,
With Robo's help, they made amazing new sounds.
From coding to building, they made quite a team,
Turning dreams into reality with a magical gleam.
So remember this tale of the robot so smart,
That friendship and tech can create a great art.
With creativity and joy, let your ideas take flight,
For imagination can turn darkness into light.

Explanation:

This poem tells the story of a child who befriends a robot, and together they explore the exciting world of technology and creativity.

Finding the Robot: The child discovers a robot in a garage, and the robot introduces itself with a friendly greeting.

Exploring Technology: The child and the robot embark on adventures, creating cool gadgets, flying drones, and exploring tech wonders.

Learning and Creating: Through their adventures, the child learns about technology and creativity, discovering how they can work together to create amazing things.

Lesson in Imagination: The poem highlights that with creativity and imagination, exciting and wonderful things can be achieved, turning dreams into reality.

The poem encourages children to embrace technology and creativity with enthusiasm and curiosity, showing that with a bit of imagination and teamwork, they can achieve amazing things.

28. The Friendly Witch

In a quaint little village, not too far away,
Lived a friendly old witch who brightened each day.
With a broomstick so shiny and a hat that would twirl,
She used her magic to help every boy and girl.
Her name was Willa, and she had a kind heart,
With spells and enchantments, she'd play her part.
When a child had a problem or needed some cheer,
Willa would listen and always be near.
One day, a young girl lost her favorite toy,
And her heart felt so sad, it was hard to enjoy.
Willa waved her wand with a sparkle and hum,
And the toy appeared with a magical thrum.
When the school was too noisy, and the class was a mess,
Willa made sure the noise turned into a jest.
With a flick of her wand, she brought peace and fun,
And soon the classroom was filled with smiles, one by one.
She showed the children how to be kind and wise,
With creativity and love in their eyes.
Willa taught them that magic isn't just spells,
But the kindness and joy that each person tells.
So remember the tale of the witch with a heart,
Who used her magic to play a kind part.
With creativity and kindness as your guide,
You can solve problems and help others with pride.

Explanation:

This poem is about a friendly witch named Willa who helps children with her magical powers, teaching them important lessons along the way.

The Friendly Witch: Willa the witch is known for her kindness and magical abilities. She uses her powers to help children with their problems.

Helping with Problems: Willa helps a girl find her lost toy and makes a noisy classroom calm and fun.

Lessons Learned: Through her actions, Willa teaches the children that magic is not just about spells, but also about kindness and creativity.

Motivational Message: The poem encourages children to embrace kindness and creativity in their own lives, showing that they can make a positive difference and solve problems with these qualities.

The poem highlights the value of helping others, being creative, and showing kindness, using the character of the friendly witch as a role model.

29. The Jungle Safari

In a jungle so lush and green,
A child set off on an adventure unseen.
With a hat on their head and binoculars tight,
They were ready to explore from morning to night.
Through thick vines and tall, grand trees,
The child moved softly with the greatest of ease.
They spotted a tiger with stripes so bright,
Sleeping in the shade, what a beautiful sight!
Next came a monkey, swinging with glee,
Jumping from branch to branch, as quick as can be.
It chattered and played, having so much fun,
Its antics and laughter brightened the sun.
Then, in a clearing, a majestic giraffe,
With a neck so long, it made the child laugh.
It nibbled on leaves from the tallest of trees,
And watched the child with curious ease.
The child learned about each animal's home,
Where they lived, how they played, and how they roamed.
The parrots' colors, the elephants' might,
All painted a picture of jungle delight.
The safari taught lessons, both big and small,
About respecting the jungle and caring for all.
The child saw that every creature has a place,
In this grand jungle, with its own special space.
So remember this journey through the green and the wild,
With respect and wonder, like a curious child.
Explore with an open heart and eyes so wide,
For nature's great wonders are yours to find.

Explanation:
This poem is about a child going on a jungle safari and discovering the fascinating animals and their habitats.

Adventure Begins: The child starts their jungle exploration, equipped and excited for the adventure.

Animal Encounters: The child sees various animals like a tiger, a playful monkey, and a tall giraffe, learning about their behaviors and homes.

Lessons Learned: The safari teaches the child about respecting and caring for the jungle and its inhabitants, understanding that each animal has a unique role.

Motivational Message: The poem encourages children to explore nature with curiosity and respect, appreciating the beauty and importance of every creature in their environment.

The poem highlights the excitement of discovering new things in nature and the importance of being respectful and mindful of the world around us.

30. The Snow Day

When winter's magic turns the world to white,
A snowstorm blankets everything in sight.
The town wakes up to a sparkling wonderland,
Where snowflakes dance and the snowmen stand.
Kids rush outside with hats and scarves so bright,
Ready for snowball fights, oh what a sight!
Laughter and giggles fill the chilly air,
As snowballs fly and everyone's there.
They build snowmen tall with buttons for eyes,
And give them warm scarves under snowy skies.
With carrot noses and hats on their heads,
The snowmen stand proudly, looking quite fed.
After the fun, it's time for a treat,
Hot cocoa with marshmallows, oh so sweet!
They sip from their mugs, with smiles so wide,
Warming up by the fire, feeling cozy inside.
The snow day is special, a winter's delight,
Filled with joy and wonder from morning to night.
It shows us the magic that winter can bring,
And the simple pleasures that snowflakes can sing.
So when the snow comes, let your heart be light,
Enjoy the snow day with pure delight.
With snowball fights and cocoa in hand,
You'll find winter's magic is truly grand.

Explanation:
This poem describes a magical snow day when a town is transformed into a winter wonderland by a snowstorm.
Winter Wonderland: The poem begins with a description of the snowstorm turning the town into a beautiful, snowy landscape.
Snow Fun: Children go outside to play, engaging in snowball fights and building snowmen, enjoying the snowy day.

Hot Cocoa: After playing in the snow, they warm up with hot cocoa and marshmallows, adding to the day's cozy and joyful experience.

Motivational Message: The poem encourages children to embrace and enjoy the simple pleasures of winter, finding joy and magic in snowy days.

The poem highlights the fun and delight of snow days, emphasizing the happiness that comes from enjoying winter activities and spending time with friends and family.

31. The Magical School

In a land where dreams and magic intertwine,
There's a special school that's truly divine.
With wands and spells and a touch of wonder,
Learning here feels like a grand adventure.
The classroom walls are alive with glee,
Where books float and sing, as happy as can be.
The teacher's lessons are full of surprise,
With potions that sparkle and magic that flies.
In math class, numbers leap and dance,
With magical creatures that prance and prance.
History's tales come to life with a flash,
As dragons and knights share stories with a crash.
Science is fun with experiments so bright,
Mixing up colors and making things light.
In art class, paints are full of delight,
Creating new worlds that shine so bright.
At recess, the playground's a magical space,
Where swings and slides are a thrilling race.
The friends you make are as magical too,
With laughter and joy in everything you do.
The school's not just lessons, it's where you grow,
With every new day, there's more to know.
Adventure and learning go hand in hand,
In this magical school, where dreams are grand.
So if you ever hear of a school that's this bright,
Remember the magic and learn with delight.
For every new lesson is a journey so sweet,
In the magical school where dreams and learning meet.

Explanation:
This poem is about a magical school where learning is filled with adventure and excitement.

Magical Classroom: The school is special, with magical elements like floating books and spell-filled lessons.

Exciting Lessons: Subjects like math, history, and science come alive with magic, making learning fun and engaging.

Playground Fun: Recess is also magical, with thrilling playground equipment and new friends to enjoy.

Motivational Message: The poem encourages children to embrace learning as an exciting adventure and to appreciate the magic of discovering new things.

The poem highlights the joy and wonder of learning in a magical setting, making education an exciting and memorable journey.

32. The Balloon Ride

Up, up, and away in a balloon so grand,
A child takes flight over a colorful land.
With a basket so cozy and a balloon so high,
They drift through the clouds and soar through the sky.
First, they glide over a forest so green,
Where trees stand tall and the leaves softly gleam.
Squirrels and birds play hide and seek,
In the emerald canopy, so lush and unique.
Next, they float over the vast, deep blue sea,
Where waves dance and sparkle with wild, joyful glee.
Ships sail below with sails full of breeze,
As dolphins leap high with effortless ease.
Then, the mountains rise, majestic and tall,
With snowy peaks that shimmer and call.
The valleys below are dotted with flowers,
As the child marvels at nature's grand towers.
From high up above, the world looks so small,
With rivers like ribbons and cities like dolls.
The child feels a wonder, so deep and so true,
At the beauty and magic the world can imbue.
The balloon ride ends, and they softly descend,
With memories and dreams they'll always defend.
For they've seen the world from a magical height,
And learned that beauty shines in every sight.
So if ever you dream of a ride in the sky,
Remember the wonders that wait up high.
With a heart full of dreams and eyes open wide,
The world's endless beauty you'll surely find.

Explanation:
This poem is about a child taking a hot air balloon ride and discovering the beauty of the world from above.

Balloon Adventure: The child takes a magical ride in a hot air balloon, exploring different landscapes from the sky.

Forest, Ocean, and Mountains: They see the lush forest, sparkling ocean, and majestic mountains, each offering its beauty.

Wonder and Discovery: From high up, the world appears small and wonderful, inspiring awe and appreciation.

Motivational Message: The poem encourages children to dream big and appreciate the beauty in the world, reminding them that magic and wonder can be found in every corner of life.

The poem celebrates the thrill of adventure and the joy of discovering the world's beauty from a new perspective, fostering a sense of wonder and curiosity.

33. The Friendly Giant

In a village snug and small,
Lived a gentle giant, kind to all.
With a smile so warm and a heart so true,
He helped the village in all he'd do.
When the river ran low and the fields turned dry,
The giant stepped in, reaching for the sky.
He lifted big buckets from the distant lake,
Pouring fresh water for the village's sake.
When the wind blew hard and the roofs flew away,
He used his big hands to fix them right away.
With gentle care, he worked through the night,
Making sure every home was safe and tight.
Children would play at his giant feet,
As he told them stories so warm and sweet.
He'd dance and laugh in the village square,
Spreading joy and kindness everywhere.
One day the village threw a grand feast,
To thank their giant, their friend, and their beast.
They cooked and danced and sang with cheer,
Grateful for the giant, who was always near.
The giant showed them with every kind deed,
That even the biggest can help those in need.
His kindness and care made the village bloom,
Filling their hearts with love and room.
So remember the giant, so gentle and wise,
Whose kindness brought tears to many eyes.
For in every heart, no matter how grand,
Kindness and love can always stand.

Explanation:
This poem tells the story of a gentle giant who helps a village in need, showing that kindness can come from the most unexpected places.

Gentle Giant: The giant is kind and helpful, using his strength to aid the village in various ways.

Helping Hands: He assists with practical problems like providing water and repairing roofs, showing his care for the community.

Joy and Gratitude: The village shows their appreciation with a grand feast, celebrating the giant's kindness and friendship.

Motivational Message: The poem highlights that kindness can come from anyone, no matter their size or appearance and that even the smallest acts of love can make a big difference.

The poem emphasizes the value of kindness and generosity, demonstrating that helping others can create a positive impact and bring people together.

34. The Butterfly Garden

In a garden where the flowers sway,
Butterflies flutter in the light of day.
Colors of every shade and hue,
Dance on wings of red, green, and blue.
From tiny eggs, they start so small,
On leaves and flowers, they softly crawl.
With patience and time, they spin a cocoon,
Dreaming of flight beneath the moon.
As days pass by, the magic unfolds,
From their cozy homes, the butterflies roll.
They spread their wings with patterns so bright,
And take to the skies in pure delight.
The garden fills with a magical scene,
Where butterflies flutter and gently gleam.
Children watch with eyes open wide,
As the butterflies dance and glide.
They learn about change from these creatures so free,
That growing and transforming is part of life's spree.
Just like the butterflies, we all have a chance,
To spread our own wings and join in the dance.
So when you see butterflies in a garden so grand,
Remember their journey, and take a stand.
Embrace the changes, let your spirit fly,
For beauty and growth are up in the sky.
In the garden of life, you'll always find,
That change is a gift to cherish and bind.
So spread your own wings and soar through the air,
With the grace of a butterfly, beyond compare.

Explanation:
This poem is about a garden full of colorful butterflies, and what they can teach us about transformation and the beauty of nature.

Butterfly Garden: The garden is a vibrant place where butterflies of all colors flutter and bring joy.

Life Cycle: The poem describes the butterfly's life cycle, from tiny eggs to the magical moment they emerge with beautiful wings.

A lesson in Transformation: Children learn that just like butterflies, they too will go through changes and growth.

Motivational Message: The poem encourages children to embrace change and see it as a beautiful part of life, inspiring them to spread their wings and grow.

The poem highlights the wonder of nature and the important lesson that transformation and growth are wonderful and necessary parts of life.

35. The Mermaid's Tale

In the deep blue sea where the waves softly sway,
A mermaid with a tail of shimmering jade,
Invited a child to dive below,
To a magical world where the sea creatures glow.
"Come with me," said the mermaid with a twinkle in her eye,
"To explore the ocean where wonders lie.
We'll swim with the dolphins and play with the fish,
In a world so vibrant, a dream to cherish."
They glided past corals in colors so bright,
Where sea anemones danced in the soft, gentle light.
Sea turtles with wisdom and starfish with grace,
Welcomed the child with smiles on their face.
The mermaid showed wonders of seashells and pearls,
And how the ocean sings as it swirls and twirls.
But she also shared a message, so heartfelt and clear,
"Protect our home, the ocean so dear."
"Keep it clean and safe from trash and decay,
For the ocean's our treasure, our world's bright display.
We need to care for the creatures who live in the deep,
To ensure their home is clean and their futures we keep."
The child listened closely, with eyes open wide,
Understanding the ocean's needs and feeling the tide.
They promised the mermaid to protect and to share,
The ocean's true beauty with love and care.
So remember the tale of the mermaid so true,
And the wonders of the ocean beneath skies so blue.
Take care of our seas, and you'll surely find,
A world full of magic and a heart so kind.

Explanation:
This poem tells the story of a mermaid who takes a child on an underwater adventure, showing the beauty of the ocean and the importance of protecting it.

Underwater Adventure: The mermaid invites the child to explore the vibrant and magical world under the sea.

Ocean's Beauty: They see colorful corals, graceful sea creatures, and the wonders of the ocean's depths.

Message of Protection: The mermaid explains the importance of keeping the ocean clean and safe from pollution.

Motivational Message: The poem encourages children to care for the ocean and its inhabitants, highlighting that protecting our environment is crucial for preserving its beauty and magic.

The poem emphasizes the importance of environmental stewardship and inspires children to take action to protect our oceans.

36. The Haunted House

In a house so old and full of creaks,
Where shadows play and the moonlight sneaks,
Children heard a story that made them quiver,
Of a haunted house by the shivering river.
They tiptoed in with hearts so brave,
To solve the mystery that made them rave.
Inside they found not a ghostly fright,
But friendly spirits with a twinkling light.
"Welcome, dear friends!" the ghosts did cheer,
"We've been waiting for you to come here.
This house is not scary, it's full of fun,
With hidden treasures for everyone!"
They showed the children the creaky old floors,
Where secret compartments held magical stores.
A map to the attic and keys to the rooms,
Each corner revealed delightful surprises and blooms.
They laughed and played with the friendly crew,
Finding treasures and secrets as they wandered through.
In the basement, they found a chest with gold,
And in the attic, a storybook of tales untold.
The ghosts weren't scary, they were kind and sweet,
And the haunted house was a wonderful treat.
The children learned with each step they took,
That sometimes what's feared is just a fun book.
So if you hear of a haunted place,
Don't fear the shadows or the eerie face.
For often you'll find, in a house that's old,
A world of adventure and treasures of gold.

Explanation:
This poem tells the story of a haunted house that turns out to be an exciting adventure with friendly ghosts and hidden treasures.

Haunted House: The house is thought to be scary, but the children are brave and decide to explore it.

Friendly Ghosts: They find that the ghosts are friendly and excited to show them around.

Hidden Treasures: The children discover magical items and secret compartments, making their adventure thrilling.

Lesson of Adventure: The poem teaches that things that seem frightening at first can turn out to be fun and full of surprises.

The poem encourages children to face their fears with courage and curiosity, showing that sometimes, what seems scary can lead to wonderful discoveries and exciting adventures.

37. The Magic Carpet

On a sunny day, a child found a rug,
In a dusty old shop, with a soft, gentle hug.
It shimmered and sparkled with colors so bright,
And whispered, "Come fly, let's take to the night!"
With a sprinkle of magic and a gentle command,
The carpet lifted up, soaring over the land.
They flew through the sky, with the wind in their hair,
Off on an adventure, far beyond compare.
First, they landed in a desert so grand,
Where pyramids sparkled in the golden sand.
They danced with the camels and marveled at sights,
Underneath the vast, starry desert nights.
Next, they soared over jungles so lush and green,
With monkeys and parrots in a vibrant scene.
They met with the locals and tasted sweet fruits,
And danced to the rhythms of drums and flutes.
From there, they flew to snowy peaks high,
Where they built snowmen and watched eagles fly.
They slid down the mountains, their laughter so free,
And felt the cold wind as it danced through the trees.
Their journey continued through cities so bright,
Where lights sparkled like stars in the cool of the night.
They saw every culture, each one unique,
And learned many wonders with every new peak.
Finally, they returned to their own cozy bed,
With dreams full of magic and wonders ahead.
The magic carpet had shown them the way,
To cherish the world, each and every day.
So if you find a rug that sparkles and gleams,
Hold tight to your dreams and follow your dreams.
For adventure awaits on a magical ride,
With a world full of wonders waiting inside.

Explanation:

This poem is about a magical carpet that takes a child on a global adventure, allowing them to explore different cultures and landscapes.

Magical Carpet: The child finds a flying carpet that takes them on an exciting journey around the world.

Global Adventure: They visit various places like deserts, jungles, snowy mountains, and vibrant cities.

Cultural Exploration: The child experiences different cultures, meets new people, and learns about the unique beauty of each place.

Motivational Message: The poem encourages children to cherish the world's diversity and embrace their dreams of adventure.

The poem inspires children to be curious about the world, appreciate different cultures, and dream big, knowing that exciting adventures and new experiences await them.

38. The Treasure Hunt

In a sunny town with streets so bright,
A group of friends set out with delight.
With maps in their hands and clues in their heads,
They started a hunt with adventurous threads.
"Find the treasure!" the map did say,
"Look high and low, let's start today!"
They searched in the park where swings sway free,
And under the big old oak tree.
They found a small box by the slide so tall,
Filled with shiny stickers and a funny little ball.
"Great job!" they cheered as they laughed with glee,
But the hunt wasn't over; there was more to see.
Next, they searched by the fountain that splashes and sprays,
And under the bench where the birds like to play.
They uncovered a bottle with a message so neat,
"To find the next clue, go where friends meet!"
They ran to the corner café with a cheer,
Where the clue led them to a treasure so dear.
A jar of colorful marbles and a note that read,
"The real treasure is the fun we've had instead!"
The friends laughed and hugged as the sun set low,
Realizing the joy in the journey they'd know.
They had found the true treasure, a bond that would last,
And memories made in the joyful past.
So when you go hunting for treasure so bright,
Remember the fun, the laughter, and light.
For the joy of discovery and friends you hold dear,
Is the greatest treasure of the whole year.

Explanation:
This poem describes a treasure hunt adventure where friends search for hidden treasures around their neighborhood and discover that the true treasure is the joy of their experience together.

Treasure Hunt: The friends follow clues on a map to find hidden treasures in their neighborhood.

Discoveries: They find small prizes like stickers and marbles, and each clue leads them to another spot.

True Treasure: The final message reveals that the real treasure is the fun they have and the friendships they cherish.

Motivational Message: The poem teaches that the joy of adventure and spending time with friends is more valuable than material prizes.

The poem encourages children to enjoy the process of discovery and treasure the experiences and friendships they make along the way.

39. The Superhero Squad

In a town so bright with skies of blue,
A superhero squad of kids formed and grew.
With capes and masks and powers so grand,
They used their gifts to help the land.
There was Speedy Sam, who ran so fast,
And Captain Grace, who could make things last.
Bright Bella could light up the night,
And Wise Max had knowledge so bright.
One day, a storm swept through the town,
Making the streets and skies frown.
Speedy Sam dashed to clear the way,
While Captain Grace helped the town to stay.
Bright Bella lit up the darkened skies,
Guiding lost people with her glowing eyes.
Wise Max offered advice to all,
Helping everyone to stand tall.
The team worked together, side by side,
Braving the storm with courage and pride.
They fixed what was broken and helped those in need,
Showing that teamwork was the best kind of deed.
When the skies cleared and the sun shone bright,
The squad celebrated their heroic night.
They knew that their powers, big or small,
Were best when used to help others and stand tall.
So remember this tale of the Superhero Squad,
That even the smallest powers can be a gift from God.
With teamwork and bravery, you'll always find,
That helping others is truly one of a kind.

Explanation:
This poem is about a group of young superheroes who use their special powers to help their town during a storm, showing the importance of teamwork and bravery.

Superhero Squad: A group of kids with unique powers who team up to make a difference.

Using Powers: Each superhero uses their abilities to address different problems caused by a storm.

Teamwork: The heroes work together to solve the issues and help their community.

Motivational Message: The poem highlights that even small acts of bravery and working together can have a big impact.

The poem encourages children to value teamwork, use their strengths to help others and be brave in the face of challenges.

40. The Secret Cave

In a meadow green and wild,
Lived a curious, adventurous child.
One day they found, behind a tree,
A hidden cave as dark as can be.
With a lantern's glow and heart so bold,
They stepped inside, where stories are told.
The cave was grand, with walls of stone,
And ancient secrets waiting to be known.
They found a map with riddles and clues,
And followed them with excited views.
Through tunnels twisty and chambers wide,
The child explored with a friend by their side.
In the heart of the cave, a treasure lay,
Gold and jewels in a golden display.
But the real treasure, shiny and bright,
Was the adventure and wonder of the night.
They discovered old scrolls with tales so grand,
Of heroes and legends from a far-off land.
With each new find, their joy did grow,
And they knew the cave held more than gold.
When they left the cave with hearts full of cheer,
They felt proud and brave without any fear.
The secret cave had taught them so,
That the best treasures are those we grow.
So if you find a cave, dark and deep,
With secrets and treasures that make your heart leap,
Remember the joy and wonder it brings,
Are the true treasures hidden in its wings.

Explanation:
This poem tells the story of a child who discovers a hidden cave full of ancient secrets and treasures.
Discovery: The child finds a secret cave and decides to explore it.

Adventure: Inside the cave, they follow clues, find treasures, and learn about ancient stories.

True Treasure: While the gold and jewels are exciting, the real treasure is the adventure and the joy of discovery.

Motivational Message: The poem teaches that the most valuable things are the experiences and knowledge we gain from our adventures, not just material possessions.

The poem encourages children to embrace curiosity, value experiences, and understand that the true treasure lies in the journey and discoveries they make along the way.

41. The Friendly Alien

One night when the stars were shining bright,
A spaceship landed with a gentle light.
Out stepped a being with greenish skin,
A friendly alien with a wide, warm grin.
The alien waved with a cheerful "Hello!"
And children gathered, excited to know.
With twinkling eyes and a curious heart,
They welcomed their visitor, ready to start.
The alien showed them the stars and the moon,
Telling tales of space in a lively tune.
They spoke of planets that danced and spun,
And comets that streaked across the sun.
The children learned of the Milky Way,
And how different worlds are not far away.
They saw the beauty in the cosmic sea,
And learned that space holds mysteries.
They shared stories of Earth and played games so grand,
Showing the alien their own special land.
In return, the alien shared tales so new,
Of galaxies far and skies of blue.
As the spaceship prepared for a starry flight,
The children waved, their hearts shining bright.
The alien taught them to see with new eyes,
That acceptance and friendship are universal ties.
So if you meet someone from far and wide,
Remember the fun of the cosmic ride.
Embrace the new with an open heart,
And welcome friends who are worlds apart.

Explanation:
This poem is about a friendly alien who visits Earth and teaches children about space and the importance of acceptance and friendship.
Alien Visit: An alien lands on Earth and greets the children warmly.

Learning about Space: The alien shares fascinating facts about space, planets, and stars.

Exchange of Stories: The children teach the aliens about their world, and in return, the aliens share stories from space.

True Message: The poem highlights that meeting new beings and embracing their differences can lead to exciting friendships and broaden our understanding of the universe.

The poem encourages children to be open to new experiences, accept differences, and understand that friendship and learning can come from anywhere, even from the farthest reaches of space.

42. The Candy Factory

Step right up to a world so sweet,
Where candy dreams and magic meet.
In a factory where wonders begin,
A tour awaits with a sugary spin.
Through candy doors and a gumdrop gate,
Children enter and can hardly wait.
The walls are lined with lollipops tall,
And chocolate rivers that sparkle and call.
The floor is made of sugar so fine,
With jellybean bushes that brightly shine.
Gumdrops grow on trees, oh so sweet,
And cotton candy clouds float above their feet.
They see how candy is made with care,
From candy canes to taffy so rare.
Machines that twirl and whirl with delight,
Creating treats that dazzle the night.
The children taste a world of cheer,
With flavors that tickle the tongue and ear.
Marshmallow mountains and caramel streams,
Make every bite feel like a dream.
The tour ends with a sweet goodbye,
As children leave with a twinkle in their eye.
They learned that magic is real, not a myth,
In a world where sweets and dreams both exist.
So remember this tale of the candy delight,
That magic can be found in the sweetest bite.
Adventure and joy are always near,
In every treat, let your dreams appear.

Explanation:
This poem takes children on a whimsical tour of a magical candy factory, where they see and taste an array of sweets and treats.

Magical Factory: The poem describes a candy factory filled with fantastical candy creations and wonders.
Sweet Delights: Children explore various candy-themed elements like lollipop walls, chocolate rivers, and sugar floors.
Learning and Fun: They learn how candies are made and enjoy tasting different treats.
Magic and Joy: The poem ends with the message that magic and adventure can be found in everyday joys, like sweets.
The poem encourages children to embrace their sense of wonder and find delight in simple pleasures, showing that magic can be discovered in the most delightful and unexpected places.

43. The Magic Shoes

In a little shop with a cozy light,
Were shoes that sparkled so shiny and bright.
A child found a pair with a magical gleam,
And slipped them on, ready to dream.
With a wish and a hop, the shoes took flight,
To lands of wonder, from morning to night.
They danced through meadows with rainbow trails,
And sailed on ships with fairy tales.
The shoes leaped over mountains so high,
And soared through clouds in the sky.
They whisked the child to a dragon's lair,
Where they found a friend with a shimmering stare.
In enchanted forests, they chased moonbeams,
And played with stars in sparkling streams.
They visited castles with golden towers,
And gardens blooming with magical flowers.
Each adventure taught the child one thing,
That magic starts with believing.
It's not the shoes, but the dreams inside,
That make every journey a magical ride.
So if you find shoes that sparkle and gleam,
Remember it's you who can make dreams beam.
Believe in your heart, let your spirit choose,
For magic is real in the magic shoes.

Explanation:

This poem is about a pair of magical shoes that take a child on fantastic adventures. The child discovers that the true magic lies in believing in oneself.
Magical Shoes: The poem begins with a child finding a pair of shoes that have magical powers.
Exciting Adventures: The shoes take the child on various adventures, including dancing in meadows, sailing with fairies, and visiting magical places.

Learning the Lesson: Through these adventures, the child learns that magic comes from believing in oneself and the dreams one holds.

Message: The poem concludes by reinforcing that real magic is not just in the shoes but in the child's belief and imagination.

The poem encourages children to believe in themselves and their dreams, showing that magic is not just found in magical objects but in the power of their imagination and belief.

44. The Flying Bicycle

In a quiet town, not far away,
A child found a bike with wings one day.
Not just any bike, but one that could soar,
To skies and clouds and so much more.
With a pedal and a cheer, up it went,
Through fluffy clouds where the rainbows are bent.
The city below seemed tiny and small,
As the bike flew high over rooftops and all.
They glided past birds with a joyful song,
And danced with the wind all day long.
The child saw the world from a brand new view,
With sights and wonders that were fresh and new.
They flew over mountains and valleys wide,
Across golden fields and the ocean's tide.
They saw distant lands and stars so bright,
With the moon as a guide in the gentle night.
Every day was a grand adventure ride,
With the flying bike as their trusted guide.
They learned to dream big and always believe,
That magic and wonder you can achieve.
So if you find a bike with wings so true,
Know that magic and dreams come from you.
Believe in your heart and reach for the sky,
With a flying bike, you can always fly high.

Explanation:
This poem tells the story of a magical flying bicycle that takes a child on incredible adventures above the city and beyond.
Magical Bicycle: The poem starts with a child discovering a bicycle that can fly.
High-Flying Adventures: The bike takes the child on exciting journeys through the sky, offering new perspectives of the world.
Exploration and Learning: The child experiences the beauty of different landscapes and learns that dreaming big can lead to wonderful adventures.

Message: The poem concludes with the idea that magic and wonder come from within, and believing in oneself makes dreams come true.

The poem encourages children to embrace their imagination, believe in their dreams, and know that with a little belief, they can reach new heights and explore the world in magical ways.

45. The Princess and the Frog

In a castle with towers tall and grand,
Lived a princess with a sparkling band.
One day by the pond, with lilies bright,
She met a frog who hopped in the light.
This frog had dreams of a royal life,
But in the pond, he felt a bit of strife.
The princess smiled and gave a cheer,
"Let's have an adventure, come over here!"
So off they went on a magical quest,
With the frog in a crown and the princess dressed.
They sailed on boats with golden sails,
And followed maps with secret trails.
They explored forests where trees would sing,
And danced with fairies in a moonlit ring.
They solved riddles in enchanted caves,
And swam with dolphins in magical waves.
Through laughter and joy, they learned anew,
That friendship is special and dreams come true.
The frog and the princess, side by side,
Found that adventure is a wonderful ride.
No need for spells or magic charms,
When true friendship has open arms.
So remember this tale of the princess and frog,
And cherish your friends like a warm, cozy log.

Explanation:
This poem reimagines the classic fairy tale of the princess and the frog, turning it into a story of friendship and adventure.
New Friendship: The story begins with a princess meeting a frog who dreams of a royal life.
Magical Adventures: Together, they embark on exciting adventures, from sailing with golden sails to dancing with fairies and exploring enchanted places.

Learning and Joy: Through their adventures, they discover that the true magic lies in friendship and sharing joyful experiences.

Message: The poem ends by emphasizing that real friendship doesn't need magical spells but is something special that makes life's adventures memorable. The poem encourages children to value and cherish their friendships, showing that true magic comes from the connections and adventures shared with friends.

46. The Secret Garden

In a place where sunlight softly beams,
A secret garden hides in dreams.
Behind a gate with flowers bright,
Is a magical world full of light.
The princess of the garden, a child so kind,
Found the gate and a path she did find.
With a gentle touch and a curious heart,
She stepped inside and found a magical start.
The roses spoke with voices sweet,
Telling stories of the summer heat.
The daisies danced in the morning sun,
And the butterflies sang as they fluttered and spun.
A wise old owl perched on a tree,
Shared tales of wonders and the secrets of the sea.
Squirrels with tiny hats and coats,
Waved hello with little notes.
The brook sang songs with a bubbly cheer,
And the wind whispered dreams to hear.
The magic of the garden was clear to see,
With every leaf and buzzing bee.
The child learned to cherish this place,
Where nature's wonders fill up space.
For in the secret garden's heart,
Every creature and flower has its part.
So if you find a hidden door,
Know there's magic to explore.
Embrace the wonders, large or small,
And let the secret garden thrill you all.

Explanation:
This poem tells the story of a hidden garden filled with wonder and magic, where nature comes to life.
Discovery: A child discovers a secret garden behind a special gate.

Magical World: Inside, the flowers and animals talk and interact, creating a magical atmosphere.

Learning and Wonder: The child learns to appreciate the magic and beauty of nature, from talking roses to wise owls.

Message: The poem concludes with a message that magic and wonder can be found in hidden places, and encourages children to explore and embrace these discoveries.

The poem aims to inspire children to find and cherish the magical and beautiful aspects of the world around them, showing that wonder can be found in the most unexpected places.

47. The Animal Parade

One night while dreaming in bed so snug,
A parade of animals gave a big hug.
They marched down the street in a grand display,
Each one unique in its own special way.
First came the elephants, big and tall,
With their trunks up high, they waved to all.
Next were the giraffes, with necks so long,
They danced in the sky, singing a song.
The lions roared softly, with manes so bright,
As the monkeys swung from left to right.
The penguins waddled in a funny line,
With their tuxedo suits, they looked so fine.
The rabbits hopped with a joyful bounce,
While the turtles moved with a steady ounce.
The colorful parrots flew overhead,
Singing songs of joy as they quickly sped.
The child watched with wide, amazed eyes,
As the parade continued under moonlit skies.
Every animal, from big to small,
Showed how special and unique they all are.
In this dream, imagination took flight,
With a world where animals danced through the night.
So remember, dear child, as you lay down to sleep,
Dream big and wide; let your thoughts leap.
For the world is vast with wonders to see,
And imagination can set your dreams free.

Explanation:
This poem describes a magical dream where a parade of animals teaches a child about the diversity and fun of different species.
Dream Parade: In the child's dream, animals of various kinds participate in a lively parade.

Unique Animals: Each animal showcases its unique traits and behaviors, from the tall giraffes to the waddling penguins.

Imagination and Wonder: The poem highlights how imagination can bring joy and wonder, with animals coming to life in a magical parade.

Message: The poem encourages children to embrace their imagination and dreams, showing that the world is full of amazing things waiting to be discovered.

It aims to inspire children to value their imagination and see the beauty and uniqueness in everything around them.

48. The Pirate Ship

On a sunny day with a breeze so light,
Children boarded a ship, ready for a flight.
The pirate ship sailed on the sparkling blue,
With a crew of brave hearts and a map to pursue.
"Ahoy, mateys!" the captain cried with cheer,
"We're off to find treasure, so have no fear!"
The sails were full, and the waves were high,
As the ship cut through the sea, under the sky.
The children spotted dolphins dancing around,
And seabirds soaring with a joyful sound.
They searched for islands with a sandy shore,
And found a hidden cave with a rusty door.
Inside the cave, with shivers and thrills,
They found a chest with gold and jewels.
But the real treasure, the captain said with a grin,
Is the adventure and fun you find within.
They sailed past sunsets, so golden and bright,
And shared stories of bravery in the night.
The pirate ship journey, with laughter and cheer,
Taught them that adventure is always near.
So dream of the sea and the ships that sail,
And let your heart follow every trail.
For life's a grand adventure, waiting to be,
Filled with treasure and joy, as wide as the sea.

Explanation:
This poem tells the story of children setting sail on a pirate ship and going on an adventurous journey across the sea.
Setting Sail: The children board a pirate ship and set off on a grand adventure.
Exploring and Discovering: They encounter dolphins, and seabirds, and eventually find a hidden treasure chest.
The Real Treasure: The poem reveals that the true treasure is the adventure and joy experienced during the journey, not just the gold and jewels.

Inspiration: It encourages children to embrace adventure, seek joy in their experiences, and remember that exciting opportunities are all around them.

The poem is meant to inspire children to be adventurous, enjoy the journey of life, and appreciate the experiences that come their way.

49. The Fairy Tale Land

In a cozy nook with a book so grand,
A child took a step into Fairy Tale Land.
With a flip of the pages and a magical spin,
They entered a world where fairy tales begin.
First, they met a girl with a golden shoe,
Who danced all night at a royal ball, it's true.
She taught them that kindness and dreams can come true,
When you believe in yourself and what you can do.
Next, they saw a house made of candy and sweets,
Where a witch with a spell met them on the streets.
But with clever thinking and bravery bold,
They escaped the witch's clutches, so brave and so gold.
They journeyed with a boy who climbed up high,
To a beanstalk reaching into the sky.
With courage and heart, he faced giants so tall,
Showing that even the smallest can conquer it all.
Then, a princess and a frog, side by side,
Shared a tale of true friendship that couldn't hide.
They learned that being kind and true to your heart,
Can bring wonderful friends and a magical start.
As the book closed gently, they came back to their room,
With dreams of adventures and flowers in bloom.
Fairy Tale Land had taught them with glee,
That the magic of stories lives in you and me.
So open a book and let the tales unfold,
For every story's magic is precious and bold.
With each fairy tale, you'll learn and you'll grow,
And discover that wonder's a gift we all know.

Explanation:
This poem describes a child stepping into a book and experiencing classic fairy tales firsthand.

Entering Fairy Tale Land: The child magically enters a world where fairy tales come to life.

Classic Tales: They encounter famous stories such as Cinderella, Hansel and Gretel, Jack and the Beanstalk, and The Princess and the Frog, learning lessons from each.

Lessons Learned:

Kindness and Dreams: From Cinderella, they learn that believing in yourself and being kind can make dreams come true.

Bravery: From Hansel and Gretel, they learn that bravery and cleverness can help overcome challenges.

Courage: From Jack and the Beanstalk, they see that even the smallest person can achieve great things with courage.

Friendship: From The Princess and the Frog, they discover that being kind and true creates lasting friendships.

Returning Home: When the adventure ends, the child returns home with a deeper appreciation for the magic in stories and their potential.

The poem encourages children to embrace the lessons from fairy tales and recognize that the magic of stories and their morals can inspire and guide them in their own lives.

50. The Knight's Quest

In a land of legends, a young knight bold,
Set out on a quest for a treasure of old.
With a shining sword and a heart full of cheer,
He embarked on his journey, no doubt or fear.
Through forests deep and mountains high,
He journeyed on with a determined eye.
He faced fierce dragons and crossed rivers wide,
With courage in his heart and his friends by his side.
He climbed a tall tower where the winds did blow,
And found a wise old sage with a tale to show.
"The treasure you seek is not just gold or gem,
But the bravery and heart found within you, my friend."
So on he went with new strength in his stride,
Braving the storms and the wild countryside.
He helped those in need and showed kindness true,
Learning that the quest was about more than just due.
At last, he reached the end of his long, winding trail,
And found the treasure with a joyful exhale.
It was a chest filled with stars and a glowing light,
A reminder that his journey had been pure and right.
The young knight returned, not with riches so grand,
But with stories of bravery and a heart that did stand.
He learned that true treasure was not what he'd sought,
But the courage and kindness that he'd always brought.
So remember, dear friend, as you venture and quest,
It's the heart of a hero that shines the best.
Be brave, be kind, and hold your dreams tight,
For the true treasure is found in your inner light.

Explanation:
This poem tells the story of a young knight who embarks on a quest to find a legendary treasure.

Starting the Quest: The knight sets out with determination, ready to face challenges.

Facing Challenges: He encounters obstacles like dragons and rivers but continues bravely.

Learning from the Sage: The knight meets a wise sage who teaches him that true treasure is about bravery and inner strength, not just gold.

Helping Others: Along the way, the knight helps people and shows kindness, realizing that the journey is about more than just finding treasure.

Finding the True Treasure: In the end, he discovers that the real treasure is the courage and kindness he has shown throughout his quest.

Returning Home: The knight returns home with stories and a heart full of bravery, understanding that the true treasure was the journey itself and the lessons learned.

The poem encourages children to understand that true value comes from bravery, kindness, and the experiences gained along the way, rather than material possessions.

51. The Magic Spellbook

In a cozy corner of a dusty old shop,
A child found a spellbook, with a magical pop!
With glittering cover and pages so bright,
It promised adventures, both day and night.
"Let's try out a spell!" the child said with glee,
"To make a toy dragon dance and fly free!"
The spell was recited with a giggle and cheer,
But instead of a dragon, a tornado appeared!
Toys spun in circles, the room was a whirl,
The magic was fun, but it caused quite a swirl.
With quick thinking and laughter, the child said with might,
"Let's fix this with magic, and make everything right!"
The next spell they tried was for a bunny to hop,
But it turned into a rabbit who wouldn't stop!
The bunny hopped high and bounced off the walls,
The child chased and laughed as it made funny calls.
With patience and care, and a wave of the wand,
The child learned each spell and grew quite fond.
They discovered that magic, while fun and exciting,
Requires responsibility and careful writing.
At last, the book closed with a satisfied sigh,
The room was now tidy, the dragon back in the sky.
The child knew the lessons, both serious and bright,
That magic is special when used just right.
So remember, dear friend, when magic is near,
It's a chance for great fun, but handle it clear.
With a heart full of wonder and wisdom in tow,
You'll find that magic can help you grow.

Explanation:
This poem tells the story of a child who finds a magical spellbook and tries out various spells.

Finding the Spellbook: The child discovers a spellbook and gets excited about the magical possibilities.

First Spell Mishap: The child attempts a spell to make a toy dragon dance but accidentally creates a tornado of chaos.

Second Spell Mishap: Another spell to make a bunny hop results in an uncontrollable, bouncing rabbit.

Learning Responsibility: Through these magical mishaps, the child learns that magic is fun but requires careful handling and responsibility.

Restoring Order: The child successfully fixes the mess with the magic and understands the importance of using magic wisely.

Final Lesson: The poem concludes with a reminder that magic, while exciting, should be used thoughtfully and responsibly to truly help one grow.

The poem encourages children to understand that while magic and adventures are thrilling, they also come with responsibilities and lessons about using power wisely.

52. The Rainbow Unicorn

In a land where rainbows touch the sky,
Lived a unicorn with a mane that shimmered high.
Her mane was a rainbow, so bright and so grand,
And she loved taking children to a magical land.
One sunny morning, a child climbed aboard,
On the unicorn's back, with a heart full of awe.
"Hold on tight," said the unicorn with a gleam,
"We're off to explore a colorful dream!"
Through fluffy clouds and fields of gold,
They soared over hills, so brave and so bold.
First, they landed in a forest of light,
Where flowers sparkled, and everything was bright.
Next, they danced with the stars up high,
In a moonlit meadow where constellations fly.
The unicorn's mane left a trail of hue,
Painting the sky in every shade and view.
They met playful pixies and giants so kind,
In a land where imagination's unconfined.
With laughter and joy, they explored every glade,
Learning that dreams are meant to be made.
As the sun began to set, with colors so deep,
The unicorn and the child began to sleep.
In dreams, they flew through realms of wonder and light,
Waking with smiles from a magical flight.
So remember, dear friend, when the skies are gray,
That magic and rainbows are never far away.
With a heart full of dreams and a smile on your face,
You can find joy and adventure in any place.

Explanation:
This poem is about a magical adventure with a rainbow unicorn who takes children on exciting journeys through fantastical lands.

Magical Unicorn: The unicorn with a rainbow mane is special and can take children to magical places.

Adventure Begins: A child climbs onto the unicorn's back, ready for an adventure.

Exploring Colorful Lands: They travel through different magical places, like a sparkling forest and a starry meadow, where everything is vibrant and wonderful.

Meeting Magical Creatures: The child and unicorn meet friendly magical creatures, enjoying their time together.

Returning Home: As night falls, they return home, and the child dreams of their magical journey.

Final Lesson: The poem ends with a message that magic and adventure are always within reach, encouraging children to keep their dreams alive and find joy everywhere.

The poem is meant to inspire children to embrace their imagination, understand that magic can be found anywhere, and always carry joy and wonder in their hearts.

53. The Talking Cat

In a cozy house with a big, soft chair,
Lived a cat who could talk, and he'd love to share.
His name was Whiskers, with fur so sleek,
And he had many tales that were fun to seek.
One bright morning, with the sun shining high,
A child named Sam heard a curious cry.
"Come here, dear friend, and let's have a chat,
I'm Whiskers the cat, and I'm glad you're at!"
Sam was amazed, "A talking cat? How true!"
Whiskers purred and smiled, "I've much to show you.
Let's embark on adventures, just you and me,
And discover the wonders of the world, you'll see."
They started with a journey through a garden so wide,
Where flowers whispered secrets as they walked side by side.
Whiskers taught Sam to listen and to see,
The magic in nature, as grand as can be.
Next, they explored a forest with trees so tall,
Whiskers shared stories of creatures great and small.
They met friendly birds and playful deer,
Learning that adventure is always near.
As the sun began to set with a warm, golden glow,
Whiskers and Sam sat by the river's slow flow.
"The best adventure," Whiskers said with a grin,
"Is the joy of companionship and the fun we're in."
So remember, dear child, as you go on your way,
Curiosity and friendship make each day bright and gay.
With an open heart and a spirit so free,
You'll find joy in the simplest things, you'll see.

Explanation:
This poem is about a magical talking cat named Whiskers who takes a child named Sam on wonderful adventures.

Talking Cat: Whiskers, the cat, can talk and invite Sam to explore and learn with him.

Exploring Together: They go on adventures in a garden and a forest, discovering the magic and beauty of nature.

Learning from Whiskers: Whiskers teaches Sam about the joy of exploration, listening, and appreciating the world around them.

Joy of Companionship: The poem highlights that the best part of their adventures is the fun and friendship they share.

Final Message: The poem ends with the message that curiosity and companionship bring joy to life, encouraging children to embrace wonder and cherish their friends.

The poem aims to inspire children to be curious, enjoy the adventures around them, and appreciate the happiness that comes from good company and exploration.

54. The Secret Island

In the middle of the sea, where waves gently roll,
A secret island waits with wonders untold.
Two children, Lily and Max, set sail one fine day,
To find this hidden land where magic does play.
Their boat touched the shore of a beach so bright,
With sand that sparkled like stars in the night.
They stepped on the island, and their eyes grew wide,
For mystical creatures were waiting inside.
They met a friendly dragon with scales of gold,
Who danced through the sky and was brave and bold.
The dragon told tales of ancient and wise,
And showed them the secrets of the island's skies.
In a shimmering forest, where trees seemed to sing,
Lily and Max found a fairy queen's ring.
The fairy queen smiled and gave them a clue,
To find hidden treasures and creatures so new.
They wandered through meadows with flowers that spoke,
And rode on a unicorn that left trails of smoke.
The unicorn whinnied and showed them the way,
To a magical waterfall that sparkled all day.
As the sun began to set with a golden embrace,
Lily and Max felt a sense of grace.
They'd discovered a world full of wonders and dreams,
And learned that magic is more real than it seems.
So if you ever wonder what's out there to find,
Just let your imagination be gentle and kind.
The world is full of magic if you look and explore,
And adventures await behind every door.

Explanation:
This poem tells the story of two children, Lily and Max, who discover a secret island filled with magical creatures and wonders.

Secret Island: The island is a hidden place with fantastic sights and mythical beings.

Magical Creatures: They meet a golden dragon, a fairy queen, and a unicorn, each offering clues and adventures.

Magical Adventures: The island is full of surprises like talking flowers and a sparkling waterfall.

Discovery and Wonder: The children learn that magic is real and can be found through exploration and imagination.

Final Message: The poem encourages children to use their imagination and curiosity to discover the magic in the world around them and to embrace the adventures that life offers.

55. The Friendly Ghosts

In an old, creaky house where shadows play,
Lived friendly ghosts who came out to sway.
They floated and twirled with a giggly cheer,
Waiting for kids to come visit them here.
One day, brave Sam and little Lily came near,
To explore the old house with no hint of fear.
They walked through the rooms where the dust softly sighed,
And soon they discovered the ghosts' playful side.
The ghosts made funny faces and danced in the light,
They played peek-a-boo and whispered, "What a delight!"
With each spooky sound and each ghostly tune,
The house turned to magic under the bright full moon.
The ghosts showed the children their favorite old game,
Like floating through walls and calling their names.
They taught Sam and Lily how to laugh with delight,
And not fear the unknown, but embrace it with might.
Together they played till the moon started to fade,
The ghosts made a promise, their friendship they made.
As dawn broke the spell and the ghosts said goodbye,
Sam and Lily waved with a tear in their eye.
So if you find a house where the old shadows dwell,
Remember friendly ghosts might just be under the spell.
With laughter and friendship, they turn fear to play,
And teach us that kindness can brighten the way.

Explanation:
This poem is about two children, Sam and Lily, who visit an old house and find that the ghosts living there are friendly and playful.
Friendly Ghosts: The ghosts are not scary but are cheerful and enjoy having fun.
Playful Hauntings: The ghosts play games and make funny faces, turning the spooky atmosphere into a playful one.
Learning and Friendship: The children learn to see ghosts as friends and not to be afraid of the unknown.

Final Message: The poem encourages children to approach new or frightening experiences with curiosity and kindness, showing that even things that seem scary can be turned into joyful and friendly adventures.

56. The Flying Castle

High in the sky where the clouds like to drift,
There's a castle that soars with a magical lift.
Its towers reach up to the stars shining bright,
And inside, there's wonder from morning to night.
In this castle, knights ride on dragons with flair,
Through fluffy white clouds and crisp mountain air.
They joust and they play with a magical gleam,
In a land where the sky is the heart of the dream.
The halls are adorned with enchanted light,
And fairies with wings flit out of sight.
They sprinkle their magic and sing with delight,
Making every adventure a breathtaking flight.
Brave young explorers are welcome to stay,
In the castle above where the clouds gently sway.
With dragons and knights and friends new and old,
Every story and dream is a treasure to hold.
So if ever you wish for a sky-high quest,
Close your eyes and imagine the best.
For the flying castle is never too far,
It's right in your heart, where dreams are a star.

Explanation:

This poem describes a magical castle that floats in the clouds, filled with adventures and fantastic creatures.

Flying Castle: The castle is high up in the sky and is magical, floating among the clouds.

Knights and Dragons: Inside, knights ride dragons, creating exciting and whimsical adventures.

Magical Creatures: Fairies and other magical beings add enchantment and joy to the castle.

Invitation to Dream: The poem encourages children to imagine their magical adventures and believe that such dreams are always within reach. It highlights the power of imagination and how dreams can take them on incredible journeys.

57. The Dragon's Egg

In a forest green where the wildflowers sway,
A child found a treasure on a bright sunny day.
It was round and it sparkled with magical light,
A dragon's egg hidden, glowing so bright.
With gentle hands, the child took great care,
Keeping the egg warm and safe with love to spare.
Every day, they watched as it twinkled and shone,
And whispered sweet stories when they were alone.
As weeks turned to months, the egg gave a crack,
And out came a dragon, small and not black.
With scales of gold and eyes full of cheer,
The dragon grew strong with each passing year.
The child learned a lesson from caring so well,
That responsibility has a magical spell.
The dragon and child became friends forever,
Their bond grew strong, and they learned to be clever.
They soared through the skies, their hearts full of glee,
Discovering wonders and all that could be.
The dragon's egg taught them more than they knew,
That caring and love make dreams come true.
So if you find something special, hold it close with pride,
Nurture it well, and let your heart be your guide.
For magic and joy can grow from a spark,
When you care with your heart and light up the dark.

Explanation:
This poem tells the story of a child who finds a magical dragon's egg and learns important lessons about responsibility and the wonders of nature through their journey.
Finding the Egg: The child discovers a glowing dragon's egg in the forest.
Caring for the Egg: The child takes special care of the egg, keeping it warm and safe.

The Dragon Grows: As the egg hatches, a friendly dragon emerges, and the child learns that taking care of something brings joy and magic.

Friendship and Adventure: The child and the dragon become friends and have many adventures together, showing that love and care lead to wonderful outcomes.

Lesson: The poem emphasizes that nurturing and responsibility bring magic and happiness, teaching children the value of caring for others and their dreams.

58. The Magic Cookbook

In a kitchen bright with pots and pans,
A child found a book with magical plans.
Its cover was golden, its pages were blue,
Filled with recipes for dishes new.
"What shall we make?" the child did cheer,
Turning the pages to see what was near.
A recipe for cupcakes that danced on the tray,
And a soup that sang and swayed all day.
With a sprinkle of magic and a dash of fun,
The food came alive, oh what a run!
Cupcakes leapt and twirled in the air,
While a pie did juggle without a care.
The spaghetti swirled and made funny faces,
And the salad did flips in tasty races.
The child laughed and joined in the play,
As the dishes performed a magical ballet.
Each meal was an adventure so wild and bright,
Turning each day into pure delight.
The magic cookbook showed with each tasty treat,
That fun and laughter are what make life sweet.
So if you find a book with recipes grand,
Try a bit of magic and see where you land.
For joy and wonder can grow with each bite,
When you cook with magic and laughter in sight.

Explanation:
This poem tells the story of a child who discovers a magical cookbook that brings food to life, leading to fun and humorous adventures.
Finding the Cookbook: The child discovers a special cookbook with magical recipes.
Making Magic Food: When the child follows the recipes, the food comes to life, dancing and performing.

Adventures in Cooking: The dishes turn mealtime into a fun and magical experience.

Lesson: The poem highlights that cooking and creativity can make life joyful and full of laughter. It teaches that adding a bit of magic and fun to everyday activities can create delightful moments.

59. The Time Traveler

In a cozy room with toys and books,
A child found a watch with curious looks.
It ticked and tocked with a magical gleam,
And whispered, "Let's explore and chase a dream."
The watch began to sparkle and glow,
And off to the past, the child did go.
First stop was ancient Egypt's sands,
Where pharaohs and pyramids stood grand.
Next, the watch ticked to a knight's great quest,
In castles and armor, with swords on their chest.
The child met a king and learned how they'd fight,
And rode on a horse in the middle of the night.
Then off to space, where rockets soared,
Among stars and planets, adventures roared.
With astronauts brave and planets to see,
The child learned how vast the cosmos could be.
From medieval fairs to the moon's bright light,
The watch took the child on a thrilling flight.
Meeting heroes, inventors, and queens so wise,
And learning history's magic before their eyes.
Back in the room with a tick and a tock,
The child returned from their time-traveling walk.
With stories to tell and wonders to share,
They learned that history holds treasures rare.
So if you find a watch with a magical tone,
Remember, adventures await you alone.
For time's great secrets are there to unfold,
In the stories of history, brave and bold.

Explanation:
This poem follows a child who discovers a magical watch that can travel through time. The watch takes the child on various adventures through history:

Discovering the Watch: The child finds a special watch that starts glowing and promises exciting adventures.

Historical Journeys: The watch takes the child to different historical periods, including ancient Egypt, medieval times, and outer space.

Learning and Adventures: During these travels, the child meets famous historical figures and learns about their lives and achievements.

Returning Home: After the adventures, the child returns home with newfound knowledge and excitement about history.

Lesson: The poem teaches that history is full of fascinating stories and adventures, and exploring it can be both exciting and educational. It encourages curiosity and learning about different times and places.

60. The Animal Rescue

In a sunny park where the wildflowers grow,
A group of kids set out with hearts all aglow.
They heard of animals needing some care,
And decided to help, showing love everywhere.
A bunny was stuck in a tangled old vine,
The kids came running, quick and just in time.
With gentle hands, they freed the small critter,
And watched it hop off with a happy glitter.
Next, they found a bird with a hurt little wing,
They made a soft nest with the best care they could bring.
With kindness and patience, the bird healed with grace,
And soon it was flying high in the sky's embrace.
A kitten lost in the cold of the night,
Was found by the kids with their lanterns so bright.
They warmed up its fur with soft blankets and play,
And found it a home where it could safely stay.
As they worked together, the children would see,
How helping each other brings joy and unity.
From feeding the stray dogs to mending the fish tank,
They learned that teamwork is never a prank.
At the end of the day, with hearts full of cheer,
They knew they'd made a difference, and their mission was clear.
To love and to care is the best way to be,
And rescuing animals brings pure harmony.
So remember, dear friends, with each little deed,
Compassion and teamwork fulfill every need.
For helping each other is a joy we should share,
And caring for others shows we truly care.

Explanation:
This poem tells the story of a group of children who set out on a mission to rescue animals in need. Here's a summary of the poem:

Starting the Mission: The children hear about animals needing help and decide to take action with enthusiastic hearts.

Rescuing Animals: They help a bunny stuck in vines, a bird with a hurt wing, and a lost kitten, showing kindness and care in each case.

Learning from the Experience: Through their efforts, the children learn the importance of compassion, teamwork, and how helping others brings joy and unity.

Final Lesson: The poem concludes by emphasizing that acts of kindness and teamwork make a positive impact and are essential to showing we care about others.

Lesson: The poem teaches that helping animals and working together not only makes a difference in their lives but also brings happiness and strengthens friendships. It encourages children to be compassionate and to see the value in teamwork.

61. The Fairy Godmother

In a town where dreams fluttered in the night,
Lived a fairy godmother, full of pure light.
With a wand that sparkled and a heart full of cheer,
She made wishes come true, bringing magic near.
One day she met Timmy, who wished for some fun,
In a garden of wonders, where his laughter could run.
With a wave of her wand and a twinkling eye,
She turned his yard into a playground to the sky.
Next came sweet Lily, who wished for a friend,
To play and to laugh and with whom she could blend.
The fairy waved her wand and with a gleam and a grin,
A playful puppy appeared, ready to begin.
When Tommy wished for courage to stand up tall,
The fairy godmother answered his call.
With a sprinkle of magic and a comforting touch,
Tommy found his bravery and learned so much.
But the magic she shared wasn't just in her wand,
It was kindness and hard work that she'd truly bond.
For every wish granted, there was a lesson to see,
That kindness and effort made magic truly be.
So remember dear children, as you dream and you play,
That kindness and hard work bring magic your way.
With love in your heart and a hand that is true,
The fairy godmother's magic will live in you.
In every small act, in each kind thing you do,
You'll find that the magic is always in you.

Explanation:

This poem tells the story of a fairy godmother who helps children with their wishes. Here's a summary of the poem:

Introduction of the Fairy Godmother: The fairy godmother, who has the power to make wishes come true, is introduced as a kind and magical figure.

Helping Children: She uses her magic to grant Timmy's wish for fun, Lily's wish for a friend, and Tommy's wish for courage.

The True Magic: The poem emphasizes that the real magic comes not just from the fairy's wand, but from kindness and hard work. The fairy's actions teach the children important lessons.

Final Lesson: The poem concludes by encouraging children to remember that their acts of kindness and effort are what truly create magic in their lives.

Lesson: The poem teaches that while magical help can be wonderful, the real magic in life comes from being kind and working hard. It inspires children to act with love and effort, showing that their actions can create magical moments.

62. The Wizard's Apprentice

In a cozy, old tower with books piled high,
Lived a wise wizard with a twinkle in his eye.
He had a young apprentice, eager and bright,
Who dreamt of casting spells and magical light.
One sunny morning, the wizard said with a grin,
"Today's the day your magic journey begins!"
With a flick of his wand and a twirl of his cloak,
He taught the young apprentice how to conjure and evoke.
First came the spell for making flowers bloom,
With a whisper and a wave, a garden would zoom.
The apprentice laughed as daisies danced in the air,
And butterflies fluttered without a care.
Next was the spell for making things float,
With a chant and a shimmer, balloons would gloat.
The apprentice cheered as a teacup took flight,
And the wizard chuckled at the joyful sight.
The final spell was one of pure delight,
To make rainbows appear on a cloudy night.
With a swish and a sway, colors filled the sky,
The apprentice's eyes grew wide with a sigh.
But as the days passed, the apprentice learned well,
That magic was more than just casting a spell.
It was kindness and laughter, a heart that would give,
And the joy that you share with the way that you live.
So remember, young friends, as you dream and explore,
Magic's not just in spells, but in kindness and more.
With a heart full of wonder and a spirit so bright,
You'll create your own magic and light up the night.

Explanation:
This poem tells the story of a young apprentice learning magic from a wise wizard. Here's what it's about:

Introduction of Characters: A young, eager apprentice is introduced, ready to learn magic from a wise old wizard.

Learning Spells: The apprentice learns different spells, like making flowers bloom, making things float, and creating rainbows.

The True Lesson: Through the lessons, the apprentice discovers that true magic isn't just about spells but is found in kindness, joy, and the way you live your life.

Final Message: The poem concludes by encouraging children to find magic in their actions and to share joy and kindness.

Lesson: The poem teaches that while magic is exciting and fun, the real magic in life comes from being kind and joyful. It inspires children to use their talents and hearts to create magic in the world.

63. The Mermaid Lagoon

In a shimmering lagoon where the sunlight gleams,
Lived mermaids who danced in the water's bright beams.
With tails that sparkled and voices so sweet,
They sang songs of magic where the sea and sky meet.
One sunny day, a child wandered near,
To the lagoon where the mermaids swam clear.
With a splash and a smile, the mermaids did say,
"Come join us, dear friend, for a magical day!"
The child dove in with a giggle and cheer,
To explore the lagoon with no hint of fear.
They swam with dolphins, and sea turtles so wise,
And watched the bright jellyfish dance 'neath the skies.
The mermaids taught lessons with laughter and grace,
About kindness and friendship, and finding your place.
They showed that in friendship, both big and small,
Everyone's special, and there's room for us all.
As the sun began setting and stars sparkled bright,
The child and the mermaids said their goodnights.
With a promise to return and play once again,
The child waved goodbye to their new mermaid friends.
So remember, young dreamers, wherever you go,
Friendship and kindness make your heart glow.
Just like the mermaids in the lagoon so blue,
Share joy and love in all that you do.

Explanation:

This poem describes a magical adventure in a lagoon filled with mermaids:
Introduction to the Lagoon: The poem begins by introducing a magical lagoon where mermaids live and play.
The Adventure: A child visits the lagoon, joining the mermaids in their underwater adventures.
Lessons Learned: The mermaids teach the child about kindness, friendship, and the importance of everyone having a special place.

Conclusion: As the day ends, the child says goodbye to the mermaids, promising to return and share more adventures.

Lesson: The poem teaches children that true magic is found in friendship and kindness. It encourages them to share joy and love with others, just as the mermaids do in their magical lagoon.

64. The Treehouse Adventures

High in the branches of a giant oak,
A treehouse stands where dreams are awoke.
With a ladder that creaks and a rope swing to soar,
It's a magical spot where adventures are sure.
The children climb up with laughter and cheer,
To their secret hideout, where imagination is clear.
With a map on the wall and a telescope too,
They set off on quests where their dreams come true.
They sail on a pirate ship made of old wood,
Searching for treasure in their backyard 'hood.
They fly with dragons, with wings that can glide,
Over forests and mountains with the wind as their guide.
They solve mysteries with clues hidden tight,
Unraveling secrets from morning till night.
They rescue stuffed animals from perilous quests,
And build towering castles where magic never rests.
Through rain or sunshine, their fun never ends,
For the treehouse is home to the best of friends.
They learn to be brave, to think and to share,
In their leafy haven where dreams fill the air.
So if you find a treehouse that's high and grand,
With a little bit of magic, it's just what you planned.
Create your own adventures, let your dreams take flight,
For in your own treehouse, every day's just right.

Explanation:

This poem describes the adventures children have in a magical treehouse:
Introduction to the Treehouse: The poem starts by introducing a special treehouse high in a tree where imagination comes to life.
Adventures: The children use the treehouse for various adventures, like sailing on pirate ships, flying with dragons, solving mysteries, and rescuing stuffed animals.

Lessons Learned: The adventures help them learn bravery, problem-solving, and sharing.

Conclusion: The poem encourages children to create their adventures and embrace the magic of imagination in their special places.

Lesson: The poem teaches that imagination and creativity can turn everyday places into extraordinary adventure spots. It encourages children to explore, solve problems, and enjoy their time with friends in their special spaces.

65. The Talking Books

In a cozy corner with a magic nook,
There's a wondrous shelf of talking books.
Each one has a voice, and they all love to chat,
Telling tales of adventures with a tip of their hat.
The first book opens with a cheerful song,
And whiskers a child where dragons belong.
They ride on a dragon's back, soaring high,
Through skies painted with rainbows and cotton-candy clouds in the sky.
Another book whispers of castles and knights,
Where bravery shines in the darkest of nights.
The pages come alive with each daring quest,
Teaching courage and kindness, and being your best.
A third book giggles with a mischievous grin,
Leading to forests where magical creatures spin.
It's a world full of fairies with sparkles and light,
Where friendship and laughter make everything bright.
The last book hums of lands far and wide,
With pirates and treasure hidden deep inside.
It's a journey of wonder, where each page is a clue,
To adventures and dreams that come true just for you.
So grab a talking book and let your dreams start,
With each turn of the page, a new story will spark.
Reading becomes magic, a journey so grand,
With talking books guiding you to every land.

Explanation:

This poem is about magical books that talk and lead a child on exciting adventures:

Introduction to Talking Books: The poem starts by introducing a special shelf of books that talk and love to share stories.

Adventures in Different Books: Each book takes the child on a unique adventure—riding dragons, joining knights, exploring magical forests, and searching for treasure.

Lessons and Fun: Through these adventures, the books teach bravery, kindness, friendship, and the joy of exploration.

Encouragement to Read: The poem ends by encouraging children to pick up a talking book and enjoy the magical journeys that reading can offer.

Lesson: The poem shows that reading can be an exciting adventure when books come alive with stories. It encourages children to explore new worlds and learn valuable lessons through the magic of books.

66. The Secret Passage

In an old house with creaky floors,
A hidden secret waits behind a door.
A dusty book on a shelf so high,
Holds the key to where the passage lies.
Push the book, and a wall starts to shake,
Revealing a passage that twists and makes,
A path of mystery, cool and deep,
Where shadows dance and secrets sleep.
Step inside with a heart so brave,
And down the stairs, you'll find a cave.
The walls are lined with maps and gold,
And stories of adventures untold.
In one room, you'll find a pirate's chest,
With jewels and coins from a treasure quest.
Another door opens to a magic land,
Where unicorns prance and dragons stand.
In the hidden rooms, you'll meet new friends,
A talking cat, and a wizard who sends,
You on quests that are thrilling and new,
With each discovery, your courage will grow too.
So if you find a passage in a house so old,
With secret doors and treasures untold,
Step in with wonder, let your dreams take flight,
For adventures await in the hidden night.

Explanation:

This poem tells the story of a hidden passage in an old house that leads to exciting and unexpected adventures:

Discovery of the Passage: It begins with a secret passage hidden behind a book on a shelf. Pushing the book reveals the entrance to the passage.

Journey Through the Passage: The passage leads to mysterious rooms with treasures, magical lands, and fantastic creatures.

Adventures and New Friends: In these hidden rooms, the child finds treasures, meets new friends like a talking cat and a wizard, and embarks on thrilling quests.

Encouragement to Explore: The poem ends by encouraging children to embrace curiosity and courage when they discover new things, suggesting that wonderful adventures await.

Lesson: The poem highlights the excitement of exploring the unknown and the rewards of bravery and curiosity. It inspires children to seek out new adventures and embrace the thrill of discovery.

67. The Magic Circus

Under a big top, so bright and grand,
A magic circus takes a stand.
With tents of rainbow, flags that sway,
The show begins with a grand display.
The ringmaster spins with a twinkle in his eye,
And a lion roars as it starts to fly.
The acrobats leap, with sparkles in their hair,
Soaring through the air without a care.
Elephants prance in shimmering attire,
Juggling balls that twinkle like fire.
A clown with a hat, full of tricks and cheer,
Makes balloons dance and disappear.
The magician's wand swishes with flair,
Turning rabbits into butterflies in midair.
A unicorn trots in glittery grace,
Bringing smiles to every face.
The tightrope walker, so brave and high,
Dances with stars in the moonlit sky.
The circus, a world of wonders and dreams,
Where magic flows in dazzling streams.
So step right up and take a chance,
Join the magic, and start to dance.
In this circus of wonder, you'll surely see,
That magic lives in you and me.

Explanation:
This poem describes the enchanting experience of a magic circus:
Setting the Scene: It begins with the spectacle of a magical circus, set under a brightly colored big top tent.
Magical Performers: It introduces magical performers and animals, such as a flying lion, glittering acrobats, and juggling elephants.
Enchanting Acts: The magician performs tricks, turning rabbits into butterflies, while a unicorn adds sparkle to the show.

Inspiring Adventure: The tightrope walker dances among stars, and the entire circus is portrayed as a world of dreams and wonder.

Lesson: The poem highlights the joy and excitement of experiencing magic and wonder. It encourages children to embrace their imagination and discover the magic within themselves.

68. The Friendly Monsters

In a cozy room, so quiet and tight,
Lived friendly monsters, hidden from sight.
Behind the closet door, they'd play and hide,
Waiting for a friend to come inside.
One night a child, brave and bold,
Heard whispers and giggles that were soft and cold.
With a gentle knock and a friendly cheer,
The child said, "Come out, there's nothing to fear!"
Out popped the monsters, big and small,
With funny hats and a cheerful call.
They wore striped socks and sparkly shoes,
And danced around with the happiest news.
One monster could juggle, another could sing,
While one played a drum with a playful swing.
They shared their games and showed their tricks,
And made the night feel like magic sticks.
The child laughed and played, having so much fun,
With monsters that sparkled like the morning sun.
They learned that not everything scary and old,
Is as bad as the stories that are told.
So when you hear noises in the dark of the night,
Remember the monsters can be a delight.
They might just be friends with a funny disguise,
Ready to share a joyful surprise.

Explanation:

This poem is about friendly monsters who turn out to be fun and playful companions:

Setting the Scene: It begins in a child's room where friendly monsters are hiding in the closet.

Meeting the Monsters: The child bravely invites the monsters out, discovering they are not scary but fun and cheerful.

Playful Activities: The monsters show their talents and play games, turning the night into a magical experience.

Lesson: The poem teaches that things that seem scary at first can turn out to be delightful and friendly. It encourages children to face their fears with curiosity and an open heart.

Not everything that seems frightening is bad. Sometimes, the unknown can bring unexpected joy and friendship.

69. The Little Mermaid

In the ocean deep and blue,
Where the waves dance and sing,
Lived a little mermaid with a shimmering tail,
Who loved to swim and swing.
One sunny day, a child on the shore,
Spied a splash and heard a cheer,
And found the little mermaid with a sparkling smile,
Floating gently near.
"Come and play!" the mermaid called,
"There's a world beneath the sea!
Where fish can talk and seashells sing,
And wonders wait for you and me."
They dove through coral castles grand,
And swam with dolphins in a swirl,
Exploring hidden treasure chests,
And sparkling pearls that made them twirl.
The mermaid taught the child to care,
For the sea and creatures bright,
To keep the oceans clean and clear,
And make sure they're shining bright.
Together they learned and laughed so much,
From sea anemones to whales,
And discovered that friendship's magic,
Is stronger than ocean's gales.
When it was time to say goodbye,
The child gave a happy wave,
Knowing that the sea's great wonders
Were now a part of their brave heart's cave.
So remember, kids, the sea's not far,
Just close your eyes and dream,
And you might find a mermaid friend,
In your wildest dreams and gleam.

Explanation:

This poem tells the story of a child who befriends a little mermaid and explores the wonders of the underwater world together:

Introduction to the Mermaid: The poem starts with the little mermaid living in the ocean and the child discovering her.

Adventure: The mermaid invites the child to explore underwater, where they see magical sights and have fun.

Lessons Learned: The mermaid teaches the child about the importance of caring for the ocean and its creatures.

Farewell and Reflection: The child says goodbye, but takes away the magical memories and lessons learned.

Friendships can lead to wonderful adventures and teach us important lessons. The ocean and its creatures are valuable, and taking care of them helps keep the world beautiful.

70. The Hidden Treasure

A crinkled map with edges old,
Lay hidden in a dusty chest,
With tales of treasures bright and bold,
And secrets yet to be expressed.
"Follow me!" the map did say,
"Through forests deep and mountains high,
With clues and riddles on the way,
To treasures hidden in the sky."
The children packed their bags with care,
And set out on their grand quest,
With curious hearts and spirits fair,
Determined to find what's best.
The first clue led them to a stream,
Where they learned that patience is gold,
For in the stillness of the gleam,
The next clue's whisper did unfold.
Through fields where wildflowers danced,
They learned that kindness always grows,
For with each smile and helping hand,
The path to treasure brightly shows.
In a cave with shadows long,
They found the courage deep inside,
For the darkness could not be strong,
When their brave hearts shone with pride.
At last, the final clue appeared,
On top of a hill so grand,
Where they found the treasure dear,
And realized the map was just a strand.
The real treasure was the journey long,
The friends they made, the lessons learned,
For with each clue and each new song,
Their hearts and minds had brightly burned.

So when you seek a treasure grand,
Remember what you'll find and see,
The true magic lies in the journey planned,
And the wonders of what you'll be.

Explanation:

This poem tells the story of children who follow an old map to find hidden treasures. Along the way, they face various challenges and learn valuable lessons:

Starting the Quest: The children discover a map that promises hidden treasures and set out on an adventure.

Lessons Learned: Each clue they find teaches them important values:

Patience by waiting by a stream.

Kindness in a field of wildflowers.

Courage in a dark cave.

Finding the Treasure: The final clue leads them to the treasure, but they realize that the real treasure is the lessons learned and the journey itself.

The most valuable treasures are not always physical objects. The true rewards come from the experiences, friendships, and lessons we gain along the way.

71. The Flying Bed

In a cozy room, so snug and bright,
A bed takes flight every night.
With a gentle whoosh, up it goes,
To magical places, nobody knows.
First stop: the North Pole, icy and grand,
Where polar bears roam, and snowflakes land.
We slide on ice and build a fort,
In this chilly, snowy, wintery court.
Next, we soar to forests, enchanted and green,
With trees so tall, a magical scene.
Fairies and elves, with wings so light,
Dance and play in the moon's soft light.
We fly to castles, high on a hill,
Where knights and dragons test their skill.
Brave and bold, we join the fight,
In dreams that sparkle through the night.
As dawn approaches, we head back home,
Our flying bed, no more to roam.
We snuggle down, our journey done,
Dreaming of new adventures to come.

Explanation:

The poem "The Flying Bed" is about a magical bed that takes a child on nightly adventures to amazing places. Each night, the bed flies to different exciting locations:

North Pole: A cold, snowy place with polar bears and fun activities like sliding on ice and building forts.

Enchanted Forests: Magical forests full of tall trees, fairies, and elves who dance and play.

Castles: Mighty castles with knights and dragons where the child can be brave and join in heroic adventures.

As the night ends, the bed returns home, and the child dreams of more adventures for the future. This poem encourages imagination, bravery, and the excitement of exploring new places.

72. The Magic Wand

Once upon a sunny day,
A magic wand came my way.
With a flick and a swish, it did respond,
To grant my wishes, beyond and beyond.
"First wish!" I cried, "A giant cake!"
Up it popped, for us to bake.
Chocolate, sprinkles, layers high,
We ate and laughed, oh my, oh my!
"Second wish," I said with glee,
"A friendly dragon just for me."
Out it came, with scales so bright,
We soared the skies, a wondrous sight.
"Third wish," I pondered, "What to do?"
"A talking dog, named Mr. Blue."
He told us jokes, and sang a tune,
We laughed and played all afternoon.
But then the wand, it had its say,
"Too many wishes for one day!"
So I wished for friends, to share my joy,
Together we played, each girl and boy.
With every wish, a lesson learned,
From each new twist, my heart was turned.
The magic wand, it taught me true,
That sharing dreams brings joy to you.

Explanation:

The poem "The Magic Wand" tells the story of a child who finds a magic wand that can grant wishes. With each wish, the child experiences fun and exciting adventures:

Giant Cake: The child wishes for a huge cake, and they have a great time baking and eating it, bringing lots of joy and laughter.

Friendly Dragon: The child wishes for a friendly dragon, and they fly together, enjoying an amazing adventure in the skies.

Talking Dog: The child wishes for a talking dog named Mr. Blue, who entertains them with jokes and songs, making the day full of fun.

Eventually, the wand reminds the child not to overuse it, leading to a final wish for friends to share in the adventures. This teaches the child the value of sharing and the joy it brings. The poem encourages imagination, fun, and the importance of friendship.

73. The Jungle Journey

In a jungle, wild and green,
Where trees are tall and skies serene,
Children set out, brave and free,
To see what wonders they might see.
First, they met a monkey, swinging high,
With a cheeky grin and a gleaming eye.
"Come along," he said with glee,
"I'll show you how we monkeys swing in the tree!"
Next, they saw a tiger, strong and grand,
With stripes like shadows on the sand.
"Welcome to my jungle home,"
He roared with pride, "where I freely roam."
Then they found an elephant, mighty and wise,
With big floppy ears and kind, gentle eyes.
"Join me," he said, "in the river to play,
Splashing water in the sunny day."
A parrot flew by, colors so bright,
Chattering away in the morning light.
"Listen close," he said with cheer,
"The jungle's full of sounds to hear."
Through the vines and leaves so thick,
They found a sloth, moving slow, not quick.
"Patience is key," the sloth did share,
"Take your time, show you care."
By sunset's glow, their journey done,
They'd learned so much and had great fun.
The jungle's more than what it seems,
Full of life and endless dreams.

Explanation:
The poem "The Jungle Journey" is about children exploring a jungle and meeting various exotic animals. Each encounter teaches them something new about the environment and the creatures that live there:

Monkey: The children meet a playful monkey who shows them how monkeys swing in the trees, highlighting the fun and agility of these animals.

Tiger: They encounter a proud tiger who introduces them to his home in the jungle, emphasizing the majesty and strength of tigers.

Elephant: A wise and gentle elephant invites them to play in the river, showcasing the joy and kindness of these magnificent creatures.

Parrot: A colorful parrot teaches them about the jungle's sounds, emphasizing the beauty and variety of life in the jungle.

Sloth: The children meet a slow-moving sloth who teaches them the importance of patience and care.

The poem encourages children to appreciate and learn from nature, showing that the jungle is full of life and dreams waiting to be discovered.

74. The Snowy Adventure

On a chilly winter day, crisp and bright,
Children set off, filled with delight.
Through snowy fields, they marched with cheer,
Ready for fun and wintery gear.
First, they met a snowman, tall and round,
With a carrot nose and buttons found.
"Welcome!" he said, "to my snowy land,
Where winter's magic is oh so grand."
Next, they found a sledding hill,
Zooming down gave them a thrill.
Laughter echoed through the air,
As they raced without a care.
Through the forest, white and still,
They spotted deer by a frozen rill.
Silent steps, they walked with grace,
In this peaceful, snowy place.
By a cozy cabin, warm and snug,
They stopped for cocoa, a friendly hug.
The fire's glow, so soft and bright,
Kept them warm through the winter night.
As stars twinkled in the sky,
They saw an owl flying high.
"Winter's beauty is all around,
In every snowflake, on the ground."
The snowy adventure, a wondrous sight,
Filled their hearts with pure delight.
They learned that winter, cold and bold,
Holds magic, beauty, and stories untold.

Explanation:
The poem "The Snowy Adventure" is about children exploring a snowy landscape and discovering the beauty and challenges of winter:

Snowman: The children meet a friendly snowman who welcomes them to the snowy land, highlighting the magical aspect of winter.

Sledding Hill: They enjoy the thrill of sledding down a hill, experiencing the fun and excitement of winter activities.

Forest: In the quiet forest, they observe graceful deer, learning to appreciate the peaceful and serene side of winter.

Cozy Cabin: They warm up in a cabin, drinking cocoa and enjoying the warmth of a fire, showing the comforting side of winter.

Owl: They see an owl flying high, reminding them of the beauty and wonder of winter nights.

The poem encourages children to embrace and appreciate the magic and beauty of winter, showing that even in the cold, there are many wonderful experiences and lessons to be learned.

75. The Moon Trip

In a rocket ship, sleek and bright,
We set off on a starry night.
Up we soared, to the sky so blue,
On a grand adventure, me and you.
Past the clouds and through the stars,
We traveled far, to where dreams are.
To the moon, our ship did glide,
With excitement, we could not hide.
We landed soft on lunar ground,
In a world where silence is the only sound.
With bouncing steps, so light and free,
We explored this place, you and me.
We saw craters, big and small,
And mountains that stood so tall.
Moon dust sparkled, like silver snow,
In this magical place, aglow.
We planted a flag, our mark to show,
That we were here, in the moon's soft glow.
We looked at Earth, so far away,
A beautiful sight at the end of the day.
Stars twinkled in the endless space,
As we explored this wondrous place.
We learned that dreams can take us far,
To the moon, to the stars, wherever they are.
With hearts full of wonder, we flew back home,
From the moon's bright land, where we did roam.
The moon trip taught us, clear and bright,
That the universe is full of light.

Explanation:
The poem "The Moon Trip" is about children taking an adventurous trip to the moon and discovering the mysteries and wonders of space:

Rocket Ship: The children set off in a rocket ship on a starry night, filled with excitement for their adventure.

Travel Through Space: They travel past clouds and stars, emphasizing the vastness and beauty of space.

Lunar Landing: They land softly on the moon and explore its unique landscape with bouncing steps.

Craters and Mountains: They observe the moon's craters and mountains, learning about its surface features.

Planting a Flag: They plant a flag to mark their visit, showing a sense of accomplishment.

View of Earth: They look at Earth from the moon, appreciating its beauty from a new perspective.

Stars and Space: The children are awed by the stars and the endlessness of space, learning that dreams can take them anywhere.

The poem encourages children to dream big and explore the wonders of the universe, showing that with imagination and curiosity, they can reach for the stars.

76. The Robot Adventure

In a cozy workshop, tools all around,
We built a robot, metal and sound.
With bolts and wires, gears and light,
Our new friend came to life, shining bright.
"Hello!" it beeped, with a friendly tone,
"I'm here to help, you're not alone."
We named it Sparks, our clever machine,
Ready for adventures, like none we'd seen.
First, it helped us clean our room,
With a whirr and a buzz, it chased the gloom.
Toys were sorted, books in place,
Sparks worked quickly, with style and grace.
Next, it cooked a splendid meal,
With robot skill, and stainless steel.
Pancakes flipped, soup stirred slow,
Our kitchen became a fun-filled show.
Then, Sparks showed us how to code,
With lines and loops, our knowledge flowed.
We built a game, with Sparks' aid,
Learning was fun, like a grand parade.
Off to the park, Sparks led the way,
Finding new friends, brightened our day.
It flew a kite, and caught a ball,
Sparks could truly do it all.
But best of all, we learned each day,
That innovation lights the way.
With every project, big or small,
Teamwork and dreams can conquer all.
Sparks, our robot, wise and true,
Taught us wonders, old and new.
The robot adventure, full of cheer,
Made us inventors, bold and clear.

Explanation:

The poem "The Robot Adventure" is about children building a robot friend named Sparks, leading them on exciting technological adventures and learning about innovation:

Building the Robot: The children build a robot named Sparks in their workshop, using various tools and materials.

Cleaning the Room: Sparks helps them clean their room efficiently, showcasing the robot's abilities.

Cooking a Meal: Sparks cooks a delicious meal, demonstrating its versatility and making the kitchen fun.

Learning to Code: Sparks teaches the children how to code, turning learning into an enjoyable activity.

Park Adventures: Sparks leads them to the park, where they make new friends and play games, highlighting the robot's interactive nature.

Innovation and Teamwork: Through their adventures with Sparks, the children learn about innovation, teamwork, and the joy of creating new things.

The poem encourages children to embrace technology, teamwork, and creativity, showing that with imagination and effort, they can achieve wonderful things.

77. The Dragon's Tale

In a land of myths, so far away,
Lived a dragon, grand and gray.
With shimmering scales and wings so wide,
He had a tale that he wanted to confide.
"Gather 'round," the dragon said,
As children sat, with eager heads.
"I'll tell you stories of times long past,
Of heroes, kings, and spells that last."
"Once upon a time, in a castle grand,
A brave knight ruled, with sword in hand.
He fought for justice, strong and true,
In battles fierce, and skies so blue."
"There were wizards with magic bright,
Who lit up the sky with colors at night.
They'd cast their spells, both kind and wise,
Bringing wonder to all eyes."
"In forests deep, and mountains high,
Lived creatures rare, who'd soar and fly.
From unicorns to griffins bold,
Their legends in the hearts were told."
"But amidst the magic, and the might,
Peace was the goal, the shining light.
For history teaches, as legends unfold,
That courage and kindness are worth more than gold."
"So when you read of ancient times,
Of dragon's roars and hero's chimes,
Remember the lessons, strong and clear,
Of bravery, love, and a world sincere."
The children listened, hearts alight,
With dreams of dragons, knights in flight.
For in the dragon's tale, they found,
A history rich, and wisdom profound.

Explanation:

The poem "The Dragon's Tale" is about a dragon who shares stories of ancient times with children, teaching them about history and myths:

Dragon's Story: A dragon invites children to hear tales from ancient times, setting the stage for a magical storytelling session.

Brave Knight: The Dragon tells about a brave knight who fought for justice, highlighting themes of courage and heroism.

Wizards and Magic: The story includes wizards with magical powers, adding an element of wonder and enchantment.

Mythical Creatures: The dragon describes various mythical creatures like unicorns and griffins, emphasizing the richness of legends.

Lessons of Peace: The dragon explains that the ultimate lesson from these stories is the importance of peace, courage, and kindness.

Children's Inspiration: The children are inspired by the dragon's tales, finding wisdom and dreams in the stories of history and myth.

The poem encourages children to appreciate history and myths, teaching them valuable lessons about bravery, kindness, and the richness of ancient tales.

78. The Enchanted Castle

On a hill, so high and grand,
Stood an enchanted castle in a magical land.
With towers tall and gates so wide,
A place where wonders did reside.
Children gathered, full of cheer,
Ready for adventure, far and near.
Through the gates, with eyes so bright,
They stepped into a world of pure delight.
Inside the castle, rooms galore,
Filled with secrets to explore.
A room of mirrors, shining clear,
Reflected dreams, both far and near.
A garden bloomed with flowers rare,
With colors bright and scented air.
Butterflies danced, and fairies flew,
In this garden, dreams came true.
A library, vast, with books so old,
Stories of magic and knights so bold.
The children read with eager eyes,
Learning of legends, reaching for the skies.
In the courtyard, dragons played,
With gentle hearts, they weren't afraid.
They taught the children how to soar,
On wings of dreams, forevermore.
A crystal ball, with mystic light,
Showed futures bright and hopes so right.
It whispered secrets, wise and true,
Guiding the children in all they'd do.
As sunset painted skies with gold,
The children left with tales retold.
The enchanted castle, a place of dreams,
Had shown them magic in endless streams.

They learned that wonder lies within,
In every heart, where dreams begin.
The enchanted castle, bold and bright,
Lit up their world with pure delight.

Explanation:

The poem "The Enchanted Castle" tells the story of children exploring a magical castle filled with enchantment and mystery:

Castle Setting: The poem starts by describing a grand enchanted castle on a hill, setting the stage for an adventurous tale.

Children's Adventure: Children enter the castle, excited and ready to explore its wonders.

Rooms of Wonder: The children find a room of mirrors that reflect dreams, a garden with rare flowers and fairies, and a vast library filled with magical stories.

Friendly Dragons: In the courtyard, they meet gentle dragons who teach them how to dream big and soar.

Crystal Ball: A crystal ball shows the children bright futures and guides them with wise secrets.

Lessons Learned: As the children leave at sunset, they carry with them the magic and lessons of the enchanted castle, realizing that wonder and dreams lie within their hearts.

The poem encourages children to embrace their imagination, explore new places, and believe in the magic of their dreams.

79. The Magic Forest

In a land not far, where dreams take flight,
Lies a magic forest, bathed in light.
With trees so tall, and leaves so green,
A place of wonder, like none you've seen.
Children ventured, brave and keen,
Into this forest, so serene.
Whispers of magic filled the air,
As they explored with joy and care.
First, they met a unicorn, white and bright,
With a sparkling horn, a wondrous sight.
"Welcome," it said, with eyes so kind,
"To a world where magic you'll find."
Next, they saw a talking tree,
Its branches waved so merrily.
"I've stories old, and secrets deep,
Of ancient woods where fairies sleep."
A river flowed, with waters clear,
Where mermaids sang, sweet and dear.
Their songs of wonder, filled the day,
Guiding children along their way.
In a meadow, bathed in sun,
Pixies played, having fun.
They danced and twirled, in glittery light,
A magical scene, pure delight.
Mushrooms glowed with colors bright,
Lighting up the forest night.
They formed a path, a shining way,
Leading to adventures, night and day.
By a crystal pond, they found a clue,
Reflections showed what dreams could do.
The children learned, with hearts so true,
That magic lies in all they do.

As dusk approached, stars did gleam,
The forest sparkled in moonbeam.
The magic forest, wise and grand,
Taught them wonders, hand in hand.
With hearts aglow, they journeyed back,
Filled with dreams, never lack.
For in the magic forest, vast and wide,
They found the magic deep inside.

Explanation:

The poem "The Magic Forest" is about children exploring a magical forest filled with enchanting creatures and plants, leading to a place of exploration and wonder:

Magic Forest Setting: The poem begins by describing a magical forest, setting a scene of wonder and enchantment.

Children's Adventure: The children venture into the forest, eager to explore and discover its magic.

Unicorn Encounter: They meet a kind unicorn, symbolizing the start of their magical journey.

Talking Tree: A talking tree shares stories and secrets of the forest, adding to the mystical atmosphere.

Mermaids' Song: They find a clear river where mermaids sing, guiding them and filling their adventure with wonder.

Pixies' Dance: In a sunny meadow, pixies play and dance, creating a delightful and magical scene.

Glowing Mushrooms: The children follow a path of glowing mushrooms, highlighting the forest's magical features.

Crystal Pond: By a crystal pond, reflections show the power of dreams, teaching the children that magic lies within them.

Journey Back: As they leave, they carry with them the lessons and magic of the forest, realizing that wonder and dreams are a part of who they are.

The poem encourages children to embrace their imagination, explore new places, and believe in the magic within themselves.

80. The Ghost's Secret

In an old house on a hill so steep,
Lived a friendly ghost, who never did sleep.
With a smile so bright and a heart so kind,
He loved to share secrets of times behind.
"Gather 'round," the ghost would say,
"I have stories from another day.
Of kings and queens, and knights so bold,
Of ancient times and tales untold."
He'd float through halls, so grand and wide,
With children following close, side by side.
"Once, this house was full of cheer,
With music and laughter, far and near."
"Here lived a family, loving and strong,
They taught me the value of right and wrong.
They helped their neighbors, far and wide,
With open hearts and arms spread wide."
"In the garden, there grew a tree,
Planted with care by old Granny Lee.
She told us tales of days of yore,
Of battles fought and legends more."
"Every room has a memory dear,
Of love and joy, of hope and cheer.
The secrets of the past, they do hold,
Lessons of kindness, pure as gold."
The ghost would show them an ancient book,
With pages worn from many a look.
"Read these stories, and you will see,
The importance of history."
"Remembering the past," he said with grace,
"Helps us all find our place.
The secrets I share, hold wisdom true,
To guide and help in all you do."

As the children left, with hearts so light,
They felt the warmth of the ghost's insight.
For in his tales of days gone by,
They found the courage to reach the sky.
The ghost's secret, shared with care,
Taught them history everywhere.
With memories cherished, old and new,
They learned to honor what is true.

Explanation:

The poem "The Ghost's Secret" tells the story of a friendly ghost who shares the secrets of the past with children, teaching them about history and the importance of memory:

Friendly Ghost: The poem introduces a kind and friendly ghost who lives in an old house and loves to share stories.

Gathering for Stories: The ghost invites children to hear tales of ancient times, including stories of kings, queens, and knights.

Historical Lessons: The ghost recounts memories of a loving family, a wise Granny Lee, and various historical events and lessons.

Ancient Book: The ghost shows the children an old book filled with stories that emphasize the importance of history.

Wisdom and Guidance: Through the ghost's stories, the children learn valuable lessons about kindness, courage, and the significance of remembering the past.

Cherished Memories: The poem concludes with the children feeling inspired by the ghost's tales and understanding the importance of honoring history and memories.

The poem encourages children to appreciate history, learn from the past, and cherish memories, showing that understanding where we come from can help guide us in the present and future.

81. The Pirate's Map

On a sunny day by the sparkling sea,
A pirate's map was found by me.
With a rusty mark and edges torn,
It promised treasure, adventure born.
"Ahoy!" we cried, with eyes so wide,
"We'll follow this map, with nothing to hide."
Through jungles thick and over hills so steep,
We set out on a quest, our promises to keep.
The map showed a path with clues and signs,
Through hidden caves and ancient pines.
With compass in hand and a hearty cheer,
We marched on bravely, without a fear.
First, we crossed a river, wide and strong,
With stepping stones, we danced along.
Next, a mountain, tall and grand,
We climbed with care, hand in hand.
In a cave, dark and deep,
We found a chest where secrets sleep.
With hearts pounding, we opened the lock,
To find the treasure, a golden rock.
But inside the chest, a note was there,
With words of wisdom, beyond compare.
"Bravery and cleverness," it said with grace,
"Are the true treasures in every place."
The real prize was not gold or gem,
But the courage and smarts we used to win.
The journey taught us more than we knew,
That adventure's treasure is in the things we do.
With the map in hand and hearts so bright,
We sailed back home, filled with delight.
The pirate's map had shown the way,
To lessons learned on a grand display.

Explanation:

The poem "The Pirate's Map" is about children following a pirate's map on an adventure to find hidden treasure, learning important lessons along the way:

Finding the Map: The poem starts with children discovering an old pirate's map that promises treasure and adventure.

Starting the Quest: The children embark on a journey, excited and ready to follow the map's clues.

Journey Through Challenges: They face various challenges, such as crossing a river and climbing a mountain, showing their bravery and cleverness.

Discovering the Treasure: They find a chest in a cave, which contains a golden rock and a note.

Lessons Learned: The note reveals that bravery and cleverness are the true treasures, teaching the children that the journey and the qualities they developed are more valuable than gold.

Returning Home: The children return home with new wisdom and joy, having learned that the real treasure is in the experiences and lessons from their adventure.

The poem encourages children to embrace bravery and cleverness, showing that the value of adventure lies in the lessons learned and the courage shown.

82. The Starry Night

Underneath the velvet sky so wide,
Children lay with stars as their guide.
The night was calm, the moon aglow,
A tapestry of stars put on a show.
"Look up," said one, with eyes so bright,
"To the wonders of the starry night.
Each twinkle tells a tale so grand,
Of distant worlds and far-off lands."
Stars like diamonds, shining clear,
Made constellations, patterns dear.
The Big Dipper's handle, the Orion's belt,
Stories of old, in the stars, were felt.
The Milky Way stretched far and wide,
A river of stars in the nighttime tide.
"It's a galaxy," one child said,
"A place where dreams and stars are wed."
The moon, so full, so round, and high,
Glimmered softly in the sky.
"Imagine walking on its silver plains,
Where adventure waits and magic reigns."
A shooting star streaked, swift and bright,
Leaving trails of wonder in the night.
"Make a wish," they whispered, soft and true,
For the stars hold dreams, just for you."
As the night wore on, they lay in peace,
Feeling the universe's sweet release.
They learned that the sky, so vast and deep,
Holds secrets and beauty, for all to keep.
With hearts aglow and dreams in flight,
They cherished the wonders of the starry night.
For the universe's mysteries, shining so bright,
Filled their hearts with pure delight.

Explanation:

The poem "The Starry Night" describes children spending a night under the stars, discovering the beauty and mysteries of the universe:

Setting the Scene: The children lie under the night sky, observing the stars and moon, creating a magical atmosphere.

Starry Wonders: They explore constellations and patterns in the stars, learning about famous ones like the Big Dipper and Orion's Belt.

Milky Way: They admire the Milky Way, understanding it as a vast galaxy filled with stars.

Moon's Magic: The full moon sparks their imagination, making them dream of adventures on its surface.

Shooting Star: They see a shooting star and make a wish, believing in the magic of the stars.

Lessons Learned: The night teaches them that the universe is full of beauty and secrets, which fill their hearts with joy.

The poem encourages children to appreciate the beauty of the night sky and the mysteries of the universe, inspiring them to dream big and cherish the wonders around them.

83. Memory updated

The Talking Dog
In a busy city, bright and grand,
Lived a dog with a special plan.
He could talk and walk with flair,
Leading adventures, beyond compare.
"Hello there!" the dog would say,
With a wag of his tail and a friendly sway.
"My name is Max, and I know the way,
To show you wonders, come what may."
First, he led them to a bustling square,
Where street performers danced in the air.
They clapped and laughed at every feat,
With Max as their guide, the day was sweet.
Next, they roamed through the park so green,
Where butterflies and flowers were seen.
Max taught them how to play and share,
With loyalty and love beyond compare.
At a shelter, Max paused with pride,
"To help these pets," he said, "is why I guide.
They need homes, love, and a caring friend,
And you can help, just like you'd mend."
As the sun set and the city lights glowed,
Max and the children took a final road.
He shared stories of friendship and trust,
Of adventures and dreams, and doing what's just.
Back home, with hearts full of cheer,
The children hugged Max, their friend so dear.
For through the city, with Max in tow,
They learned that true friends help you grow.
The talking dog taught them with glee,
That loyalty and friendship are the key.
In every adventure, big or small,

With friends by your side, you can conquer all.

Explanation:

The poem "The Talking Dog" is about a talking dog named Max who takes children on adventures through the city, teaching them about loyalty and friendship:

Talking Dog: Max, the talking dog, introduces himself and invites the children on an adventure.

City Adventures: They visit a city square with street performers and a park with butterflies, experiencing fun and joy.

Helping at the Shelter: Max shows the importance of helping animals at a shelter, emphasizing the value of compassion and care.

Lessons of Friendship: As the day ends, Max shares stories about the importance of loyalty and friendship.

Cherishing Friendship: The children learn that having friends and being loyal is important, and they appreciate Max's guidance.

The poem encourages children to value friendship, loyalty, and helping others, showing that these qualities lead to fulfilling adventures and personal growth.

84. The Hidden Kingdom

In a land where secrets softly gleam,
Lies a hidden kingdom, like a dream.
With magic and wonder, beyond compare,
A place where adventures fill the air.
One day, a map with a glittering glow,
Led brave children where wonders grow.
Through a forest thick and mountains high,
They found the kingdom under the sky.
The kingdom sparkled with colors bright,
With creatures dancing in pure delight.
Fairies with wings of silver and gold,
And wise old wizards with stories told.
A golden throne in the center stood,
Where the kindest ruler, wise and good,
Taught the children lessons true,
Of leadership and kindness, shining through.
"Leaders," he said, "are strong and fair,
With hearts full of love and minds that care.
Help each other, lift each soul,
That's how you lead, that's your goal."
In the garden, flowers sang a tune,
As the children learned from noon till moon.
They planted seeds and tended trees,
With laughter carried on the breeze.
They helped the creatures in their plight,
With bravery and kindness, day and night.
Through every trial, with hearts so bright,
They learned that helping makes things right.
As they bid farewell, the kingdom's light,
Guided them home through the starry night.
The hidden kingdom had shown them the way,
To lead with love and brighten each day.

With hearts of gold and spirits high,
They cherished the lessons of the sky.
For in the hidden kingdom's grand display,
They found the magic in leading the way.

Explanation:

The poem "The Hidden Kingdom" tells the story of children discovering a magical, hidden kingdom and learning valuable lessons in leadership and kindness:

Finding the Kingdom: The children find a map leading to a hidden kingdom full of magic and wonder.

Magical Creatures: They encounter fairies, wizards, and other magical beings, experiencing the beauty of the kingdom.

Lessons in Leadership: The kind ruler of the kingdom teaches the children about leadership, emphasizing fairness, kindness, and helping others.

Learning and Helping: The children engage in activities like planting and helping magical creatures, learning the importance of kindness and teamwork.

Returning Home: They leave the kingdom with newfound wisdom, understanding that leadership and kindness can make a positive impact.

The poem encourages children to embrace leadership qualities and kindness, showing that helping others and leading with a caring heart are valuable traits.

85. The Magic Amulet

In a dusty old shop, so hidden away,
A magic amulet was found one day.
With a sparkle and a glint, it shone so bright,
Promising adventures, day and night.
A child named Sam took the amulet in hand,
And felt a shiver, oh so grand.
As soon as it touched, a sparkle flew,
And suddenly, the world seemed new.
First, Sam found themselves in a land of gold,
Where mountains shimmered and tales were told.
Dragons soared with wings so wide,
And treasure chests were open wide.
Next, the amulet twinkled, leading the way,
To an underwater world, deep and gray.
With mermaids singing in oceans blue,
And dolphins dancing, their joy so true.
Then, it sparkled, and with a gleam,
Sam was in a forest, like a dream.
Trees whispered secrets of olden days,
And fairies danced in moonlit haze.
The amulet shone with magic bright,
Guiding Sam through realms of light.
From sky-high castles to ancient ruins,
Each adventure was full of tunes.
But the greatest magic Sam did see,
Was not in places, but the bravery,
And kindness found in each new quest,
In helping others and doing their best.
As the sun set, and the amulet's glow dimmed,
Sam returned home, with heart full of whim.
For the magic amulet, with powers so true,
Had shown that adventures can make dreams come true.

With every adventure, Sam learned the fact,
That magic lives in the heart's impact.
The amulet's power, so bright and grand,
Was the kindness and courage Sam would command.

Explanation:

The poem "The Magic Amulet" tells the story of a child named Sam who discovers a magical amulet that leads to exciting adventures:

Finding the Amulet: Sam finds a magic amulet in an old shop, which starts to glow and promise adventures.

First Adventure: The amulet takes Sam to a land of gold with dragons and treasure, showcasing a world of wonder.

Underwater World: The amulet then guides Sam to an underwater realm with mermaids and dolphins.

Enchanted Forest: Next, Sam visits a magical forest with talking trees and dancing fairies.

Lessons Learned: Throughout the adventures, Sam learns that the true magic lies in bravery and kindness, helping others, and doing their best.

Returning Home: Sam returns home with a heart full of joy, understanding that the real power of the amulet was in the experiences and the lessons learned.

The poem inspires children to recognize that true magic and adventure come from within—through bravery, kindness, and helping others.

86. The Rainbow Bridge

Across the sky, so wide and bright,
A rainbow bridge shines in the light.
Its colors gleam in a dazzling arc,
Inviting children to embark.
One sunny day, with hearts aglow,
They stepped onto the bridge's bow.
With every step, the colors spun,
Leading them to adventures and fun.
First, they landed in a land of sweets,
Where candy flowers and chocolate trees meet.
Lollipop lakes and gumdrop hills,
Filled the air with sugary thrills.
Next, the bridge sparkled, shifting hue,
To a world of wonder, shiny and new.
Glistening sands on a crystal shore,
With seashells singing, and waves that roar.
The bridge then led them to a starry realm,
With planets and comets at the helm.
They danced with aliens, friendly and bright,
Under the glow of the cosmic light.
In another world, so lush and green,
A forest of giants, like nothing seen.
With talking animals and trees that sway,
They learned about nature in a magical way.
As the journey continued, the bridge did bend,
Showing the beauty of worlds that blend.
Each land unique, with wonders grand,
Taught the children about the diverse strands.
When the rainbow bridge began to fade,
They returned home, where memories stayed.
With hearts enriched and eyes so wide,
They cherished the magic of the worlds inside.

For the bridge showed them, clear and bright,
That beauty and wonder are all in sight.
In every world, whether big or small,
Diversity and magic can truly enthrall.

Explanation:

The poem "The Rainbow Bridge" describes a magical bridge made of rainbow colors that leads children to different enchanting worlds:

Rainbow Bridge: The poem begins with children discovering a colorful, rainbow bridge that promises magical adventures.

Land of Sweets: The bridge first takes them to a land filled with candy and chocolate, creating a delightful experience.

Crystal Shore: Next, they visit a sparkling beach with seashells and singing waves.

Starry Realm: The bridge then leads them to a star-filled space where they dance with friendly aliens.

Lush Forest: They explore a giant forest with talking animals and learn about nature's beauty.

Lessons Learned: The journey shows the diversity and beauty of different worlds, teaching the children that every place has its magic and wonder.

The poem encourages children to appreciate the beauty and diversity of the world, highlighting that magic and wonder can be found everywhere and in every kind of place.

87. The Animal School

In a magical school where the trees grew tall,
Animals gathered for the learning hall.
With desks made of leaves and chairs of bark,
They taught their lessons from dawn till dark.
First came the owl, wise and so bright,
Teaching the class with all its might.
"Learning to read and write," it said,
"Helps you explore the world ahead."
Next, the fox with a clever grin,
Taught the art of solving problems within.
With puzzles and riddles, sharp and neat,
It showed how thinking can be a treat.
The squirrel, quick and full of cheer,
Taught skills of planning through the year.
"How to gather and store with care,
For every season and every fare."
In the gym, the lion roared with pride,
Teaching strength and courage side by side.
"To be brave and strong, you must train,
For challenges come, and you must remain."
The rabbit hopped in, gentle and kind,
Teaching the class to ease their mind.
"Relax and breathe, take it slow,
For peace and calm help you grow."
Lastly, the parrot with colors so bright,
Taught the art of speaking right.
"To share your thoughts and ideas so clear,
Helps you connect and bring others near."
As the day ended and stars shone bright,
The animals smiled with pure delight.
For in their magical school so grand,
They'd shared the gifts to help them stand.

The children learned with hearts aglow,
That learning is a way to grow.
In every lesson, big or small,
Knowledge and skills can help you stand tall.

Explanation:

The poem "The Animal School" is about a magical school where animals teach children different skills and the importance of learning:

Magical School Setting: The poem starts by introducing a school where animals teach in a magical setting with natural materials.

Owl's Lesson: The wise owl teaches reading and writing, emphasizing the importance of these skills for exploring the world.

Fox's Lesson: The clever fox teaches problem-solving through puzzles and riddles.

Squirrel's Lesson: The squirrel instructs on planning and storing resources for different seasons.

Lion's Lesson: The strong lion teaches about bravery and strength, showing how to face challenges.

Rabbit's Lesson: The gentle rabbit teaches relaxation and calming techniques.

Parrot's Lesson: The colorful parrot teaches effective communication and sharing of ideas.

The poem motivates children to value learning and developing various skills, showing that knowledge and personal growth are important for facing challenges and achieving success.

88. The Secret Garden

In a hidden corner, snug and small,
A secret garden waits for all.
With a rusty gate and ivy high,
It hides its wonders from the eye.
One sunny day, with hearts so light,
Children found the garden's sight.
With a push of the gate and a gentle creak,
They entered a world so unique.
In this garden, flowers did speak,
With voices soft and colors sleek.
"Hello there!" a daisy said with cheer,
"We've been waiting for you to appear."
A rose with petals rich and red,
Told tales of sunshine and rain it spread.
"Each drop of rain," it softly said,
"Helps us bloom and grow ahead."
Next, they met a wise old tree,
With branches wide and leaves so free.
"It's patience and time that help us rise,
To reach the stars and touch the skies."
A rabbit hopped with ears so long,
Teaching the children a hopping song.
"Joy and laughter are our guide,
In this secret garden where wonders reside."
A butterfly with wings so bright,
Showed them how to take delight.
"Life's a journey with twists and turns,
With each new day, something new you'll learn."
The garden's magic grew with time,
With every lesson, every rhyme.
The children learned to cherish and see,
The beauty of nature and its harmony.

As they left the garden's gate,
They felt their hearts rejuvenate.
For in the secret garden's grand display,
They found wonder and wisdom to light their way.

Explanation:

The poem "The Secret Garden" describes a magical garden where talking plants and animals teach children valuable lessons:

Discovering the Garden: The children find a hidden garden, excited to explore its mysteries.

Talking Flowers: They meet flowers that speak and share their stories, teaching about growth and the importance of rain.

Wise Old Tree: A tree teaches patience and time, showing how they help achieve great things.

Joyful Rabbit: The rabbit shares a song about joy and laughter, emphasizing the happiness in life.

Bright Butterfly: The butterfly teaches about delight and learning from life's journey.

Lessons and Wonders: The garden's magic and lessons help the children appreciate nature and its harmony.

The poem motivates children to explore and appreciate the beauty of nature and to understand the importance of patience, joy, and learning in their lives.

89. The Dragon's Lair

Deep in the mountains, high and grand,
Lies a dragon's lair, a hidden land.
With caves so dark and flames so bright,
It seems a place of awe and fright.
Brave children set out with hearts so bold,
To explore the tales that they had been told.
Through winding paths and rocky trails,
They journeyed on to the dragon's lair.
As they entered the cave with echoes loud,
They saw the dragon, fierce and proud.
With scales of gold and eyes of fire,
The dragon watched, their hearts grew higher.
But instead of roars and fiery breath,
The dragon spoke with a voice like a hymn.
"Welcome, young friends, to my home so deep,
Where I guard treasures and secrets I keep."
The dragon's eyes, so wise and kind,
Revealed a heart that was gentle and fine.
With a smile so warm and wings spread wide,
It offered the children a place to abide.
"Bravery," said the dragon with grace,
"Isn't just in facing fear's embrace.
It's in the kindness and courage you show,
In helping others as you go."
The children learned of treasures rare,
Not gold or jewels, but love and care.
The dragon's kindness and wisdom clear,
Taught them lessons they'd hold dear.
As they left the lair with hearts aglow,
They felt a warmth from the dragon's show.
For bravery, they knew, was not just might,
But kindness and courage in the light.

With tales to tell and memories grand,
They thanked the dragon and took a stand.
To be brave and kind, in every way,
And spread the lessons learned that day.

Explanation:
The poem "The Dragon's Lair" is about children visiting a dragon's lair and learning valuable lessons about bravery and kindness:

Journey to the Lair: The children bravely set out to explore the dragon's lair, despite it being a place of fear and awe.

Meeting the Dragon: Instead of being fierce, the dragon greets them warmly and kindly.

Lessons from the Dragon: The dragon teaches that true bravery is not just about facing fear but also about showing kindness and care to others.

Treasures of the Heart: The real treasures are not material but the love and care shared with others.

Returning Home: The children leave with new wisdom, and understanding that bravery and kindness are important qualities to embrace.

The poem encourages children to recognize that bravery involves more than facing fears; it includes being kind and caring toward others, reflecting the true essence of courage.

90. The Magic Potion

In a cozy shop with shelves so neat,
A magic potion was a special treat.
With bubbles that danced and colors bright,
It promised adventures day and night.
A child named Mia took the potion with care,
Excited for magic, beyond compare.
With a sip of the brew, so sweet and strange,
Her world began to shift and change.
First, Mia found she could fly so high,
Swooping through clouds in the big blue sky.
She soared over mountains and rivers wide,
Feeling the wind as she took a ride.
But soon the potion gave a tricky twist,
Turning her voice into a croaky hiss.
"Can't speak a word," she said with a frown,
As her words made funny sounds all around.
Then she discovered a curious gift,
Turning invisible with a swish and lift.
She sneaked through doors and vanished from sight,
Finding herself in a comical plight.
She learned to use her powers with care,
For every gift had a trick to share.
Flying was fun, but she had to land,
And invisible tricks needed a steady hand.
With each adventure, Mia saw so clear,
That special abilities came with cheer.
But being careful and thinking it through,
Made her magic adventures enjoyable too.
As the potion's effects began to fade,
Mia felt proud of the choices she made.
For the magic potion had shown her true,
That with great power, great care is due.

Explanation:

The poem "The Magic Potion" tells the story of Mia who drinks a magic potion that grants her special abilities and leads to exciting but tricky adventures:

Finding the Potion: Mia finds a magic potion that promises amazing adventures.

Flying Ability: She discovers she can fly, enjoying the freedom of the sky.

Tricky Twist: The potion causes her voice to become croaky and funny, creating some challenges.

Invisibility: Mia gains the ability to turn invisible, leading to both fun and tricky situations.

Lessons Learned: She learns that special abilities come with their own set of challenges and that using them wisely is important.

Returning to Normal: As the potion's effects wear off, Mia reflects on the experience and understands the value of care and thoughtfulness with magical gifts.

The poem encourages children to understand that while special abilities can be exciting, they also come with responsibilities and the need for careful use.

91. The Enchanted Library

In a library old and grand,
With shelves that stretch across the land,
There was magic, pure and bright,
Where books came to life with delight.
One quiet day, with a turn of a key,
The library doors swung wide with glee.
The children stepped in, eyes full of wonder,
To find the magic that they had pondered.
First, a book with a cover so blue,
Opened its pages and out they flew.
Pirates and ships from a sea so vast,
Welcomed the children to adventures fast.
They sailed on waves and found a chest,
With treasures and maps to put to the test.
They fought with dragons, fierce and strong,
And danced with fairies all day long.
Next, a book with stars so bright,
Took them to space on a thrilling flight.
They rode on comets and saw the moons,
Exploring the cosmos and singing tunes.
A tale of wizards and spells so wise,
Led them to a castle in the skies.
With potions and magic, and spells to cast,
They learned that knowledge is a spell that lasts.
In a book of nature, green and grand,
They roamed through forests and rolling sand.
They met talking animals and trees that spoke,
Learning about the world with every joke.
As the sun set and the library's light dimmed,
The books went quiet and the magic trimmed.
The children left with hearts so bright,
Knowing that adventures were within their sight.

For the enchanted library had shown them the way,
That stories and dreams can light up their day.
In every book, adventure waits,
And learning is magic that opens gates.

Explanation:
The poem "The Enchanted Library" describes a magical library where books come to life, leading to exciting adventures and learning experiences:

Discovering the Library: Children enter a grand library with magical books.

Pirate Adventure: They first explore a pirate book, sailing on ships and discovering treasures.

Space Journey: Another book takes them on a space adventure, exploring comets and moons.

Wizard Tales: They visit a wizard's world, learning that knowledge and magic are lasting gifts.

Nature Exploration: In a nature book, they learn about the environment by talking about animals and trees.

Returning Home: As the magic fades, the children leave with a newfound appreciation for stories and learning.

The poem encourages children to see the magic in books and learning, showing that adventures and valuable lessons can be found in every story.

92. The Friendly Witch's House

In a cozy corner, tucked away,
A witch's house awaited play.
With a roof of twigs and walls of charm,
It promised magic and no alarm.
One bright day, with hearts so keen,
Children ventured to this scene.
With a creak of the door and a friendly cheer,
They stepped inside, their hopes sincere.
The witch, so warm with a hat so tall,
Welcomed them in with a gentle call.
"Come in, dear friends, and take a seat,
My house is filled with magic and treats."
In the kitchen, pots bubbled and steamed,
With scents of cookies and pies that gleamed.
The witch served tea in cups of gold,
And stories of magic and wonders told.
In the living room, a cozy fire,
Warmed the space with a gentle choir.
With enchanted games and puzzles to try,
The children laughed and reached the sky.
A corner of toys and spells galore,
Kept the children wanting more.
Magic wands and hats to wear,
Made the room a fantasy fair.
The witch showed tricks with a flick of her wand,
Turning ordinary things into wonders fond.
Stars and sparkles filled the air,
As the children marveled at the magical flair.
Before they left, the witch gave a hug,
With a wink and smile, and a cozy rug.
"Remember, dear friends, magic's in sight,
In every kind word and act that's right."

With hearts full of joy and spirits bright,
The children thanked the witch that night.
For her house was a place of fun and grace,
Where friendship and magic had a warm embrace.

Explanation:

The poem "The Friendly Witch's House" is about children visiting a witch's home, where they experience fun, magic, and friendship:

Entering the Witch's House: The children find a charming witch's house and enter with excitement.

Warm Welcome: The friendly witch greets them warmly and invites them in.

Magical Kitchen: They enjoy cookies and tea in a magical kitchen with enchanting stories.

Cozy Living Room: They play games and enjoy a cozy fire in a room filled with joy.

Toys and Spells: The children explore magical toys and experience fun tricks.

Parting Gift: The witch gives them a hug and a reminder that magic and kindness are found in everyday actions.

The poem inspires children to appreciate the magic in kindness and friendship, showing that even in unexpected places, warmth and joy can be found.

93. The Pirate's Island

Far across the ocean, wild and free,
Lies a pirate's island, a mystery.
With palm trees swaying and seashells bright,
It promises adventures from morning till night.
One sunny day, with sails unfurled,
A crew of kids set off to explore the world.
They found the island with a joyful cheer,
And followed a map that led them near.
On the beach, pirates danced and sang,
With hats and swords and a clanging clang.
But these pirates were friendly and keen,
And welcomed the children to join their scene.
Together they searched for treasure so grand,
With maps and clues and a shovel in hand.
They dug through sand and climbed up trees,
Working as one with the ocean breeze.
When a puzzle arose and it seemed so tough,
The pirates and kids found teamwork enough.
They shared their ideas and combined their might,
To solve the riddle and see the light.
At last, they uncovered a chest so old,
Filled with gems and coins, and stories untold.
But the greatest treasure they found that day,
Was the joy of working in a team's display.
The pirates cheered and thanked the crew,
For together they had made dreams come true.
As the sun set and the sails were raised,
The children knew their hearts were amazed.
For on the pirate's island, bold and bright,
They learned that teamwork makes things right.
With friends and pirates, side by side,
They had found the treasure of joy and pride.

Explanation:

The poem "The Pirate's Island" is about children visiting a pirate's island and learning valuable lessons about teamwork:

Finding the Island: The children sail to a mysterious pirate island filled with adventure.

Friendly Pirates: They are greeted by friendly pirates who invite them to join in the fun.

Treasure Hunt: Together, they search for hidden treasure using maps and clues.

Teamwork: When faced with challenges, they work together, sharing ideas to solve problems.

Finding Treasure: They discover a chest filled with gems but realize that the real treasure is the teamwork they experienced.

Lessons Learned: As they leave, they understand that working together makes adventures and challenges more rewarding.

The poem encourages children to value teamwork and friendship, showing that working together can turn challenges into joyful and successful experiences.

94. The Magic Seeds

In a garden bright with sunshine's cheer,
Lived seeds so magical and dear.
Each one a promise, small and neat,
Of wondrous plants that soon would greet.
A child named Alex found a pack,
Of seeds so special, never lack.
With a sprinkle of water and a little care,
The magic began, and wonders were there.
First, a seed grew into a tree,
With rainbow leaves that danced with glee.
The children climbed and swung with joy,
In the branches high, they'd laugh and buoy.
Next, a seed became a flower fair,
With petals glowing everywhere.
It sang sweet songs with every breeze,
And swayed along with the buzzing bees.
Another seed, with a gentle sprout,
Grew a vine that twisted about.
It reached for the sky and twirled around,
Creating a playground on the ground.
Then came a plant with fruits so bright,
That sparkled like stars in the moonlight.
Each fruit held a secret to share,
Of nature's magic, beyond compare.
With every plant and every seed,
Alex learned of nature's creed.
That with a bit of love and light,
Magic grows with all its might.
The garden bloomed with colors true,
And the children learned as they grew.
That nature's magic is wondrous and free,
With lessons in every plant and tree.

As they played and learned each day,
They knew that magic was here to stay.
For the seeds they'd planted and the care they gave,
Made the garden a magical place to rave.

Explanation:
The poem "The Magic Seeds" is about a child planting magical seeds that grow into wondrous plants, leading to fun and learning about nature:

Finding the Seeds: Alex discovers a pack of magic seeds and plants them with care.

Rainbow Tree: The first seed grows into a tree with rainbow leaves, creating a joyful climbing spot.

Singing Flower: The second seed turns into a flower that sings and glows, attracting bees.

Twisting Vine: The third seed becomes a vine that twists and turns, providing a fun playground.

Sparkling Fruit: Another plant grows fruits that sparkle and reveal nature's secrets.

Lessons in Nature: Alex learns that nature's magic comes with care and love and that every plant has its own special story.

The poem motivates children to appreciate and care for nature, showing that magical things can grow from simple acts of love and attention.

95. The Talking Animals

In a meadow green with flowers bright,
Lived animals with voices light.
One sunny day, as the children came,
The animals spoke and shared their fame.
A wise old owl with feathers gray,
Said, "Come and listen, I'll tell you today.
I've watched the seasons change and pass,
From spring's soft blooms to winter's glass."
The children gathered with eager eyes,
As the owl told tales beneath the skies.
Of forests deep and stars so high,
And the quiet nights where fireflies fly.
A playful fox with a bushy tail,
Spoke of adventures, wind, and hail.
"I've chased the shadows in the light,
And danced with friends under the moon's bright."
The fox's stories were full of cheer,
Of games and fun and friends so near.
With each new tale, the children laughed,
And learned of nature's playful craft.
A gentle deer with eyes so kind,
Shared secrets of the forest's mind.
"Respect the trees and all that grows,
For every plant and creature knows."
The deer's words were soft and true,
Teaching kindness in all they do.
To care for nature and protect the land,
And always lend a helping hand.
The last to speak was a tiny mouse,
Who lived in a cozy, hidden house.
"I've learned that kindness is the key,
To friendship and joy, for you and me."

With tiny paws and a gentle voice,
The mouse showed how kindness is a choice.
To share, to help, and to understand,
Is the way to make the world so grand.
As the sun set and the stories ended,
The children felt their hearts were mended.
For the talking animals had taught them right,
That kindness and care make the world bright.

Explanation:

The poem "The Talking Animals" is about animals in a meadow who can talk and share their life stories with children, teaching important lessons:

Meeting the Owl: A wise owl shares stories of the changing seasons and the beauty of nature.

Playful Fox: A fox talks about fun adventures and games, showing the joy of playful moments.

Gentle Deer: A deer teaches the importance of respecting nature and being kind.

Tiny Mouse: A small mouse emphasizes that kindness is crucial for building friendships and joy.

Lessons Learned: The children learn that kindness, respect, and care for nature make the world a better place.

The poem encourages children to be kind, to appreciate nature, and to understand the value of friendship and caring for others.

96. The Hidden Treasure

In a forest deep and shadows long,
A map was found where dreams belong.
With clues and riddles, strange and neat,
It promised treasure and adventures sweet.
A group of friends with hearts so bright,
Set out together with great delight.
Through tangled woods and streams that flow,
They followed the map where mysteries grow.
The first clue led to an ancient tree,
Where whispers told of a secret key.
They searched and dug beneath the roots,
Finding a key with shiny boots.
With the key in hand, they moved along,
To a cave where echoes sang a song.
Inside the cave, the walls were dark,
But they found a light that left a spark.
The next clue was a puzzle old,
With pieces hidden and stories told.
Together they worked, side by side,
Until the puzzle was complete and wide.
A hidden door was revealed with care,
They opened it to a sight so rare.
Gold and jewels, a treasure grand,
But it wasn't the gold that made them stand.
For the real treasure, they learned that day,
Was the friends they had along the way.
Their laughter, their help, and every cheer,
Made the journey special, year after year.
As they left the cave with hearts so full,
They knew that the treasure was not just gold.
It was the bond they shared and the joy they found,
In each other's company and the love around.

So when you seek a treasure so bright,
Remember it's not just gold or light.
It's the friendships and memories dear,
That make every adventure a treasure near.

Explanation:

The poem "The Hidden Treasure" tells the story of a group of friends who go on a treasure hunt in a mysterious forest and discover important lessons:

Finding the Map: They find a map that leads to hidden treasure and sets off on an adventure.

Ancient Tree Clue: They find a key beneath an ancient tree using the first clue.

Cave Adventure: They explore a dark cave and solve a puzzle to reveal a hidden door.

Discovering the Treasure: They find gold and jewels but realize that the true treasure is their friendship.

Valuable Lessons: They learn that the real treasure is the joy and bond they share.

The poem encourages children to value friendships and teamwork, showing that the real treasure in life is the love and connections we build with others.

97. The Magic Shoes

In a cozy shop with shoes so bright,
A pair of shoes sparkled in the light.
With laces tied and colors grand,
They promised magic from a distant land.
A child named Lily saw them there,
With a glimmer of magic in the air.
She slipped them on and felt a whirl,
As the shoes began to twirl and twirl.
First, they took her to a castle high,
In a land where dragons flew in the sky.
She met a knight with a shining sword,
Who taught her courage and how to be adored.
Next, the shoes danced to a forest deep,
Where talking trees and fairies leap.
She learned from them to be brave and kind,
And never to leave her dreams behind.
Then, they leaped to an ocean wide,
With waves that sparkled and dolphins that glide.
Lily swam with creatures of the sea,
And learned that bravery sets your spirit free.
Through mountains tall and valleys low,
The magic shoes made her courage grow.
She climbed and soared with a heart so strong,
And discovered that courage helps you along.
As the shoes twirled back to her room,
Lily knew she'd faced each challenge and gloom.
For the magic shoes had shown her the way,
To be brave and kind, come what may.
With every step and every stride,
Lily felt the magic inside.
The shoes may rest, but the courage stayed,
And in her heart, the lessons laid.

So when you find a pair of shoes so bright,
Remember that magic's in the heart's light.
For courage and kindness are the real treasures,
In every adventure and all of life's measures.

Explanation:

The poem "The Magic Shoes" tells the story of Lily, who discovers a pair of magical shoes that take her on thrilling adventures:

Finding the Shoes: Lily finds a pair of magical shoes in a shop that promises exciting journeys.

Castle Adventure: The shoes take her to a castle where she learns about courage from a knight.

Forest Journey: She visits a magical forest where talking trees and fairies teach her bravery and kindness.

Ocean Exploration: The shoes bring her to the ocean where she swims with dolphins and learns about the freedom that courage brings.

Mountain Climb: She climbs mountains and grows braver with each step, discovering that courage helps her overcome challenges.

Returning Home: When the magic shoes return her to her room, she carries the lessons of bravery and kindness in her heart.

The poem encourages children to understand that true magic comes from within and that courage and kindness are valuable qualities for any adventure.

98. The Fairy Tale Castle

In a land where dreams and stories meet,
Stood a castle grand and sweet.
With turrets high and gates of gold,
It held adventures yet untold.
One bright morning, with hearts so true,
Children wandered in, their joy anew.
They stepped through arches, tall and grand,
Into a world of wonder, so magical and grand.
In the castle halls, so vast and bright,
Fairy tale characters danced with delight.
They met a princess with a golden crown,
Who showed them kindness all around.
The children learned from her gentle ways,
That helping others brings sunny days.
With every smile and every deed,
They saw how kindness plants a seed.
Next, they joined a brave young knight,
Who fought for justice, fair and right.
He taught them courage, strong and bold,
To face their fears and be brave as gold.
They journeyed on to meet a clever fox,
Who solved puzzles and unlocked locks.
The fox's wisdom showed them how,
To use their brains and think things through, now.
In the castle's garden, under the sun,
A magic mirror shared stories spun.
It told of heroes and lessons learned,
Of dreams pursued and respect earned.
As the day turned to twilight's glow,
The children felt their spirits grow.
For the fairy tale castle had taught them well,
That kindness, courage, and wisdom swell.

When they left, they took away,
The lessons from the castle that day.
In their hearts, they carried the light,
Of fairy tales and dreams so bright.
So remember, dear friends, when you dream or play,
Fairy tales have lessons to guide your way.
With kindness and courage, your heart will gleam,
And you'll find the magic in every dream.

Explanation:

The poem "The Fairy Tale Castle" describes children visiting a magical castle filled with fairy tale characters who teach important life lessons:

Entering the Castle: The children enter a grand castle full of wonder and magic.

Meeting the Princess: They learn from a princess about kindness and how helping others brings happiness.

Joining the Knight: They meet a brave knight who teaches them about courage and facing fears.

Meeting the Fox: A clever fox shows them the importance of using their brains and thinking through problems.

Magic Mirror: A magic mirror shares stories of heroes and the value of pursuing dreams and showing respect.

Leaving the Castle: The children leave with valuable lessons about kindness, courage, and wisdom.

The poem encourages children to embrace these fairy tale lessons in their own lives, showing that kindness, bravery, and wisdom are timeless qualities that can guide them on their journey.

99. The Dragon's Friend

In a valley green with hills so high,
Lived a dragon who soared the sky.
With scales that sparkled and wings so wide,
He looked so fierce but had a gentle side.
One day a child named Sam wandered near,
And saw the dragon without any fear.
"Hello there!" said Sam with a friendly grin,
"Do you mind if I come and visit within?"
The dragon blinked with eyes so kind,
And welcomed Sam, their hearts aligned.
Together they flew to lands so far,
Past glittering rivers and a shooting star.
In a meadow bright where wildflowers grew,
Sam learned the dragon's favorite things to do.
They played with clouds and danced with the breeze,
And laughed with the trees and honeybees.
Through forests dark and mountains steep,
They shared stories and secrets to keep.
Sam learned the dragon wasn't just a sight,
But a friend with dreams that shone so bright.
They faced challenges, both big and small,
Helping each other through every call.
When others saw the dragon's fierce face,
Sam showed them the heart of kindness and grace.
The dragon's roars were not of fright,
But songs of joy that filled the night.
With Sam by his side, the world felt new,
Full of wonders and friendships true.
When the sun set and stars came out,
Sam and the dragon gave a cheerful shout.
For they knew that understanding and care,
Turned fears to friendship, beyond compare.

So if you meet someone who seems so tough,
Remember that kindness is always enough.
A friend's heart is gentle, kind, and true,
And the magic of understanding starts with you.

Explanation:

The poem "The Dragon's Friend" tells the story of a child named Sam who befriends a dragon and learns important lessons:

Meeting the Dragon: Sam approaches the dragon without fear and is welcomed warmly.

Adventures Together: They embark on adventures, exploring new places and enjoying each other's company.

Understanding the Dragon: Sam learns that the dragon is kind and friendly, not just fierce.

Facing Challenges: They support each other through difficulties, showing that friendship helps overcome fears.

Sharing Joy: The dragon's roars are revealed to be joyful songs, and their friendship brings new experiences.

Lessons Learned: The poem teaches that understanding and kindness can transform fear into friendship.

The poem encourages children to approach others with kindness and understanding, showing that even those who seem different or frightening can become true friends.

100. The Magic Paintings

In a cozy room with walls so white,
Hung paintings that sparkled in the light.
With colors so vivid and scenes so bright,
They held secrets of magical delight.
One day a child named Jamie came,
With a curious heart and an artist's aim.
As Jamie touched a painting with care,
The scene began to shimmer and flare.
A boat on a river, so calm and clear,
Lifted Jamie up with a joyful cheer.
They sailed through waves with a gentle breeze,
Past islands of treasure and singing trees.
In another frame with a castle grand,
Jamie stepped into a fairyland.
With knights and dragons, both fierce and kind,
They joined the adventures that they'd find.
A meadow of flowers with petals so wide,
Became a place where Jamie could glide.
Dancing with butterflies and a rainbow or two,
Jamie painted their dreams in colors so true.
In a jungle scene with wild and free,
Jamie swung with monkeys from tree to tree.
They painted the sunset and stars so high,
And made a new world beneath the sky.
Each painting brought a new delight,
With wonders to explore both day and night.
Jamie learned that creativity's the key,
To making dreams and magic come to be.
When the day ended and the room grew still,
Jamie felt a joy that couldn't be still.
For the magic of painting and imagination's art,
Had painted a smile deep in Jamie's heart.

So when you pick up colors and brushes bright,
Let your imagination take its flight.
For with each stroke and every line,
You'll find adventures and dreams that shine.

Explanation:

The poem "The Magic Paintings" describes how Jamie discovers that paintings in a room come to life, leading to exciting adventures and creative joy:

Discovering the Paintings: Jamie finds paintings that sparkle with magic.

Sailing Adventure: Jamie touches a painting of a boat and sails through a magical river.

Fairyland Castle: Another painting takes Jamie to a fairyland with knights and dragons.

Meadow Fun: Jamie dances with butterflies in a meadow painting.

Jungle Joy: A jungle painting allows Jamie to swing with monkeys and explore.

Creativity's Power: Jamie learns that creativity brings dreams to life and brings joy.

The poem encourages children to use their imagination and creativity, showing that art can lead to wonderful adventures and deep personal joy.

Milton Keynes UK
Ingram Content Group UK Ltd.
UKHW031033020824
446373UK00001B/95